Get Recruited For A

Football Scholarship

What 9th, 10th, 11th and 12th Graders Need To Do

Lynn West &
Athletic Scholarship Info

Copyright © 2013

Lanie Dills Publishing
ISBN 0916744132

Additional Books by Athletic Scholarship Info

Introduction

While there are other types of scholarships that can either pay or help pay for your son's college education such as scholastic scholarships, if your high school football player has a reasonable amount of talent, there is an excellent chance that he could be recruited to play college football on either a full ride or a partial athletic scholarship.

These football scholarships are very lucrative; many of them are valued in excess of $150,000 and even more depending on the school. Full ride scholarships pay for tuition, meals, room and board and tutoring among other things. And now, in accordance with new NCAA rulings, some schools are offering four-year full ride scholarships.

Partial scholarships may pay for any number of a combination of expenses, but do not cover everything. Of course, everyone wants to obtain one of the full ride types, but not all schools are required to offer them; only the top level of schools have to offer the full ride type, so the majority of colleges offer some variation of the partial scholarship. Often partial football scholarships are combined with other types of scholarships to ensure that all your son's college expenses are met.

There are some several thousand colleges in the U.S. that offer football scholarships, so if your son follows a proven plan such as the one clearly taught in this book, there is a very good chance that he will be offered an athletic scholarship to play football at the collegiate level somewhere.

The recruiting process, which consists of developing into the kind of player the college coaches are looking for and getting the coaches to notice your son's talent is a marathon rather than a sprint. It helps to start early, even as early as the 9th grade to start doing the things necessary to get on the radar of the college coaches. "Get Recruited For A Football Scholarship What 9th,

10th, 11th, 12th Graders Need To Do" gives you a no nonsense step-by-step plan presented in monthly increments so that you do not become overwhelmed with the total recruiting process all at once.

For example, if your son is a junior, he will be instructed on a monthly basis about what he should be doing that particular month in the recruiting process. You, as parents will also be given incite and instructions about what you can do to help with contact Emails, recruiting profiles, highlight videos, and personal athletic websites – all essential elements of a successful recruiting campaign.

There are many myths surrounding the recruiting process. For example, many parents still think that if their son is good enough, the college coaches will come banging his door down. In fact, this is far from the truth. While there are a few (100 –150) hot elite players in the country every year that will almost automatically be recruited, they are certainly not the norm.

By far, most of the other thousands of high school football athletes and their parents will have to be proactive in the recruiting process. This means that you will have to be instrumental in getting the coaches to notice your son. If one of these scholarships is your dream, then you cannot afford to sit back and wait for the coaches to find you. For one thing, most of them do not have the recruiting budget to travel around looking for talent. They depend on you making contact with them first.

This book, in simple to understand language, guides you through the recruiting process from the 9th grade through the 12th grade and it also ensures that you stay compliant with the NCAA rules. With this book, you will never be alone as you navigate the process. In fact, you will have a recruiting expert with you at all times.

Website: http://college-athletic-scholarship.com
Facebook: https://www.facebook.com/CollegeAthleticScholarship
Twitter: @GuruRecruiter
YouTube: http://www.youtube.com/gururecruiter

Get Recruited For A..1
Football Scholarship 1
Introduction..2
Chapter 1..9
FRESHMEN ~ SEPTEMBER..9
Chapter 2..11
FRESHMEN ~ OCTOBER 11
Chapter 3..15
FRESHMEN ~ NOVEMBER 15
Chapter 4..18
FRESHMEN ~ DECEMBER 18
Chapter 5..21
FRESHMEN ~ JANUARY 21
Chapter 6..25
FRESHMEN ~ FEBRUARY 25
Chapter 7..28
FRESHMEN ~ MARCH 28
Chapter 8..31
FRESHMEN – APRIL 31
Chapter 9..35
FRESHMEN ~ MAY 35
Chapter 10..40
SOPHOMORE ~ SEPTEMBER 40
Chapter 11..43
SOPHOMORE ~ OCTOBER...43
Chapter 12..46
SOPHOMORE ~ NOVEMBER 46
Chapter 13..51
SOPHOMORE ~ DECEMBER...51
Chapter 14..54
SOPHOMORE ~ JANUARY 54
Chapter 15..58
SOPHOMORE ~ FEBRUARY 58
Chapter 16..62
SOPHOMORE ~ MARCH..62
Chapter 17..65
SOPHOMORE ~ APRIL 65
Chapter 18..69

SOPHOMORE ~ MAY 69

Chapter 19..71

SOPHOMORE ~ SUMMER VACATION (Time To Get Ahead)
....71

Chapter 20..75

JUNIOR ~ SEPTEMBER 75

Chapter 21..80

JUNIOR ~ OCTOBER 80

Chapter 22..84

JUNIOR ~ NOVEMBER..84

Chapter 23..89

JUNIOR ~ DECEMBER 89

Chapter 24..93

JUNIOR ~ JANUARY 93

Chapter 25..96

JUNIOR ~ FEBRUARY 96

Chapter 26..101

JUNIOR ~ MARCH 101

Chapter 27..104

JUNIOR ~ APRIL 104

Chapter 28..109

JUNIOR ~ MAY..109

Chapter 29..111

JUNIOR ~ SUMMER VACATION..111

Chapter 30..114

SENIOR ~ SEPTEMBER...114

Chapter 31..119

SENIOR ~ OCTOBER 119

Chapter 32..123

SENIOR ~ NOVEMBER 123

Chapter 33..127

SENIOR ~ DECEMBER 127

Chapter 34..131

SENIOR ~ JANUARY 131

Chapter 35..136

SENIOR ~ FEBRUARY 136

Chapter 36..140

SENIOR ~ MARCH 140

Chapter 37..143

SENIOR ~ APRIL 143
Chapter 38 146
SENIOR ~ MAY 146
APPENDIX A 149
Letter of Introduction or Initial Contact Email 149
APPENDIX B 151
Sample Recruiting Profile: 151
APPENDIX C 152
Tracking Sheet: 152
APPENDIX D 153
Highlight Video Information: 153
APPENDIX E 156
Letters Of Recommendation For Your College Application 156
APPENDIX F 158
General College Preparation: 158
APPENDIX G 160
Personal Website 160
Thank You! 161

What 9th Graders Need To Do

Many people advise that the high school freshmen year is really too early to begin thinking about playing football in college, but from our many years of experience of helping thousands of student/athletes realize their dream of playing college sports, we strongly disagree.

Even in the ninth grade, there are a number of things you can do to start setting the stage properly to ensure that when the time comes you are in contention for a college football scholarship.

One of the most important things you can do as you begin your high school career is to determine to maintain an acceptable GPA. Grades are something that can easily gradually slip below a score that most colleges will accept.

Whether you obtain a sports scholarship or not, in most cases, you will not be admitted to college without having good grades. They do not have to be great grades, but they do have to be the minimum that each school requires. Some schools require a higher GPA than others, so be sure to know the GPA requirement of each school on your wish list.

Even as a freshman, there are some things you can do to help get yourself recruited? Remember, the recruiting process for college sports is a marathon rather than a sprint. There are certain steps that you should take throughout the entire four years of high school. The steps you take as a freshman are foundational steps that will only serve to make your entire recruiting process successful.

That's what this book is all about. We've arranged it from month to month so that you can accomplish each month's suggestions before going on to the next.

Chapter 1

FRESHMEN ~ SEPTEMBER

You Are Now A "Student/Athlete"

Congratulations! According to the NCAA, beginning with the 9th grade, you are no longer just a student, but you have achieved the status of *"Student/Athlete."* You can now start officially preparing for your college sports career.

If you want, you can now register with the **NCAA Eligibility Center.** You don't have to register this year, but it is never too early and you'll have it done and behind you. You can register online at:

This book is designed to separate you from your competition in the eyes of the college football scouts and coaches. While there are many tens of thousands of high school football players across the nation, ONLY the top 100 – 150 are actively recruited by the big schools.

The truth is the vast majority of colleges don't have the funds, time or the recruiting staff to heavily pursue football recruiting. This is bad news for them, but very good news for you since you can be instrumental and proactive in securing your football scholarship.

Don't worry; the recruiting process is actually simple and fairly easy to do if you accomplish the steps incrementally as you go along. Putting things off or failing to take action will only hurt your scholarship chances.

You'll have at hand all the tools and information you will need every step of the way. However, in order for you to have the best opportunity to be recruited, it will be your responsibility to follow through and actually take action at each stage of the recruiting process.

It is our main goal to help you land a college football scholarship at a school of your choosing. **Begin this month researching various colleges** and comparing the differences in the schools in terms of academics, athletics, location, campus environment, size and whether or not they are public or private institutions.

Chapter 2

FRESHMEN ~ OCTOBER

Are You Really Football Recruiting Material?
It's a tough question to ask, but it is a necessary one. Take a moment to answer the following five questions. Honestly answer and see how you measure up.

1. Do you have the basic skills and natural ability?
2. Do you have a solid knowledge of the sport?
3. How is your overall body strength and speed?
4. Do you possess the mental fortitude to handle the grueling demands of the game?

5. Do you have what it takes to play football in college?

Sincerely asking yourself these difficult questions now and doing a complete realistic assessment of yourself as it relates to football will help you spot weaknesses so that you can begin early to improve in those areas.

The fact is, unless you are one of those rare elite and mature athletes, as a freshman, you will not be seeing much playing time. Most coaches, even those coaching at smaller schools, hesitate to bring up freshmen players, and **as many as 95% of freshman do not see any significant varsity play.**

Does that mean you won't have a chance at a Division I scholarship? Absolutely not, there is still a GREAT CHANCE that you will, provided you **start early to improve your game and market yourself to the coaches**.

If you are one of the exceptional stellar 'blue chip' athletes, and after your freshman year you have the stats to back it up, by all means, send an email to the college football coaches where you would be interested in playing. Doing so will get you in the database of the coaches. If you do not have substantial stats after your freshman football season, there are two schools of thought:
- Wait until next year to contact the coaches when you so have playing stats.
- Go ahead and send the introductory email just to get on the radar this year.

The advantage of getting on the college coaches radar early is that they can have a full four years to watch as you improve your stats and game.

Most high school athletes dream of playing for one of the big time D-I Universities; however, the truth is, that very few athletes have the God-given talent to play at this highly competitive level, but for those of **you who don't, there are still many, many opportunities** for you to play and earn yourself a college scholarship.

While hard work, heart, passion, and persistence can get you far, at some point the reality of your physical attributes do set in. Remember the old adage, "you can't teach height?" You're a high school freshman and you will, more than likely get taller, but **the point is be realistic in your physical assessment** of yourself.

For example, you may not have the physical attributes to play at the University Of Alabama, but the coach at University Of Memphis and literally hundreds of other schools would love to recruit you for his team.

Due to improved training methods and conditioning techniques, **today's athletes are stronger and faster than ever before**, and they begin their football training at an earlier age. In fact, in some sports, basketball for example, scholarships are being offered even to eighth graders.

You'll be competing for scholarships with athletes from all over the globe. Your talents will be compared with athletes all across the U.S. and around the world. Do all you can to improve yourself, and when you've done all you can, bear in mind that **during the recruiting process the athlete's *Potential* is a vital consideration.** College coaches know from experience that even moderate athletic performance can be boosted immensely with their intensive training methods.

Here are some things you can do this month to prepare to play scholarship level football:

Research the different schools where you would like to play to determine what athletic level you need to be to play football at those schools.
Start **grooming yourself to eventually compete** at those schools. Set your sights on becoming the kind of athlete they recruit for their teams.

Also, start doing research to see what kind of **grades and SAT/ACT** scores you will need to be admitted to those schools.

This is not premature; every grade you make this year will go toward your final GPA, a very important consideration for college admittance committees.

Remember, according to the NCAA, you are no longer just a student; you are now a **student athlete**. For the most part, recruited athletes **have and maintain good grades**.

Chapter 3

FRESHMEN ~ NOVEMBER

Avoid these 10 Deadly Recruiting Mistakes:
Even as a freshman, if you expect to be recruited to play college football, avoid these ten mistakes during your high school football career.

1. *Dismiss or downplay attention from the coaching staff at any college.* You may think that you have the potential to play at a Division I school, however be courteous and respectful of any attention from any level school. You've got four years to go and you don't ever know what's in the future. Keep your options open.

2. *Lie about recruiting attention.* The truth will come out eventually. Sure everyone wants to feel important, but just stick to the truth.

3. *Develop a negative relationship with your high school football coach*. Your high school coach will be the first person after your parents that a college coach will call. If you've been difficult to get along with in high school, what college coach would want you?

4. *Display bad sportsmanship*. Again, the college coaches will hear about this during their recruiting investigation.

5. *Skip practices and team meetings*. This behavior in high school shows the college coaches that you don't approach your commitments seriously.

6. *Disrespect your parents and teachers*. This behavior indicates that you really don't respect others and will more than likely continue this attitude in college.

7. *Act like you are better than your teammates*. Why would any college football coach want to recruit an athlete who treats his teammates badly?

8. *Get in trouble off the field*. Keep your nose clean. Coaches do not want to recruit trouble to their teams.

9. *Mouth off to the officials*. Just stick to your game and resist the urge to talk back to the officials.

10. *Neglect your schoolwork*. Keep your grades up from your freshman year through your senior year. Coaches will be looking at your GPA, which will include all your grades, even these early freshman grades.

NOTE: If you have been fortunate enough to rack up some significant varsity stats this season, wait until your season is completely over and then contact the coaches where you think you would like to play football. (Only do this if you have been a raging standout)

- Sending them either a letter of introduction or an initial contact email with your recruiting profile attached and a link to your highlight video makes the initial contact.

NOTE: Instructions and samples for all of these are in the Appendix at the back of this book.

Chapter 4

FRESHMEN ~ DECEMBER

The Case For Playing Multiple Sports
Freshmen sometimes have difficulty looking down the road and planning their high school years academically and athletically to achieve the best advantage in their recruiting process later on. This is where your parents, coaches, teachers and guidance counselors can be of tremendous help.

**As strange as it may sound, playing multiple sports in high school can really help you to be recruited to play college football. Here's why:

**Athletes who play and do well in more than one sport *typically have that competitive spirit* that is needed to play at the collegiate level.

Student athletes who play multiple sports are **generally more well rounded and as a rule they possess the competitive heart that is required to play on college football teams.

Playing more that one sport shows that you enjoy competing year-round and not just during the football season. This is a **good way to get noticed by the college scouts and coaches.

Competing in more than one sport **teaches you early on how to compete. Obviously, the more you compete, the better you get at competing. This is a skill that carries over from sport to sport.

Competing in multiple sports gives you many **more opportunities to succeed in difficult high-pressure situations. This will give the coaches more opportunities to see who you are and what you can do.

Playing in more than one sport helps you tremendously to **develop mental toughness.

Things you learn in competition can't be taught on the practice field or by hitting the weights. Playing multiple sports lets you keep your **competitive edge all year long. When you play only one sport, there is a tendency to get complacent during the off-season.

College football **coaches are attracted to multiple sport athletes that constantly challenge themselves to improve their competitive edge.

You may have heard that the smart thing to do is focus your attention on one high school sport, but as you can see there are many advantages to playing more than one.
Something else to keep in your mind is that many, many athletes have actually been recruited to play one of their alternate sports instead of football

Things College Football Coaches Wish You Knew:

It would make the coach's *job a lot easier if you would educate yourself about how things really work as the recruiting process* unfolds for you. Here are some things you should remember as you begin to actively be in the process.

Stop thinking right now that your grades are not important. Coaches no longer recruit risky athletes, and with the recent changes in the NCAA's GPA requirements, this trend will only continue.

Don't assume that just because you are a good player, the coaches will recruit you. The coaches must know about you before you can be on their radar. *YOU must let them know that you are interested in their school and football program.* This can be done by sending a letter or email of introduction to the coach, or by filling out a questionnaire that he may have sent. They EXPECT you to make the initial contact with them.

Do not think that a camp invite means you are being recruited. These camp invites are sent out by the hundreds and sometimes even thousands. The camps raise revenue for the athletic programs and sometimes for the football coaches too. The same invite is sent to everyone, but there only a few players that are actually being recruited.
That being said, however, since the camps are run by college coaches and their assistants, this could be a great opportunity for you to show them what you can do and turn yourself into a recruiting prospect.
Today, almost everyone has a Facebook or some other social network account. *Be aware that college coaches can find out a lot about your background from visiting your pages on these websites.* Don't allow anything on them that you wouldn't want a coach to see.

December Is A Great Month To Work On Fitness
This month, start to earnestly work off the field on you physical fitness. As you become more fit, notice how your athletic performance naturally improves.

Chapter 5

FRESHMEN ~ JANUARY

How To Get Some Respect:
Take advantage of the winter months to build muscle mass and to also focus on increasing muscle strength.

Respect doesn't just automatically happen on the football field, you have to earn it by putting in the ultimate weight room effort in the off-season.

Can anyone out train you? This is a question you should honestly ask yourself. Some of your teammates may have the edge as far as talent goes, but you can make up for it by giving your all in the weight room.

Believe it or not, games are won or lost during the off-season. With that in mind, it is time to get serious about your resistance training.

Bigger muscles are not always stronger muscles. Our goal this month is to not only continue building your muscle mass, but to also increase your muscle strength.

Exactly What Is Strength?

Strength is your ability to overcome resistance, and it is needed to improve quickness, agility, coordination, resistance to injury, increase bone density, and it also helps develop stronger muscles.

So, as you can see, it is much more than just building bulky muscles. In fact, bulky muscles often result in decreased agility, finesse and speed.

Blow Your Competition Away Next Year

If you want to leave your competition in the dust next football season, then it is totally essential that you take your strength training seriously as it is the foundation for developing muscular endurance, flexibility, acceleration, agility, mobility and maximum speed.

The hard truth is that your performance on the field is largely determined by how powerful you are. Explosive power is a combination of strength and speed. So, as you can see, strength training is one of the most important elements in your overall football training.

How To Do Reps

Establish the right way to do reps now to obtain the most benefit from your time on the weights. Pay close attention to how you are performing your reps. It is critical that you use the right form in every rep. Use full control, complete each exercise intelligently and apply full range of motion. You have not actually completed a rep unless you have performed it in strict form.

Jerking or throwing a weight up does not count.
Remember, only you know whether you are giving your best during this period of your training. When you are facing down a competitor next season, *make sure you know in your own mind that you have left nothing in the weight room.*

20 Important Character Traits For College Football Recruits:
College football coaches look for other attributes besides athletic talent when evaluating potential recruits for their football teams.

Even if you are not an 'elite' or 'blue chip' athlete, but you are an above average player with decent grades, test scores, and you also *possess most of the following characteristics, you will have an excellent chance to be widely considered for a football scholarship:*

1. You have drive
2. You are aggressive
3. You have determination
4. You are conscientious
5. You are self-motivated
6. You are capable of building trust
7. You have leadership abilities
8. You are respectful
9. You are disciplined
10. You are emotionally controlled
11. You are hard-working
12. You are team oriented
13. You are competitive
14. You are mentally tough
15. You are friendly and outgoing
16. You are committed to excellence
17. You have a positive attitude
18. You are responsible
19. You are coachable
20. You display good sportsmanship

Take a good look at this list of the twenty personal characteristics that coaches routinely consider in their potential recruits and honestly see how you size up. If you think you are weak in any of these areas, commit NOW to improve while your high school career is basically still ahead of you.

Chapter 6

FRESHMEN ~ FEBRUARY

When To Start The Recruiting Process?
More than 95% of Freshman will not have had any varsity playing time by the end of their freshman season, but for those of you that did get called up to actually see playing time and you also have impressive stats, you can begin now to send your recruiting information to colleges where you would like to play football. Doing this will get you on the radar for recruiting at those schools, and it will allow you the excuse to send periodic updates of your accomplishments.

"Here's What To Include..."
Send an introductory email or letter with a .doc or .pdf attachment of your athletic or recruiting profile and a link to your highlight video, which you have posted either on your personal athletic website or on YouTube.

NOTE: Instructions and samples for all of these can be found in the Appendix at the back of this book.

Most of you will not be doing this until after your junior season has ended, but a few will have substantial stats after their sophomore year and there will also be a rare few that will have impressive stats after their freshman season.

If you don't see playing time until your junior season, don't be discouraged, many athletes go on to play Division I football coming from this particular situation.

Speed And Football

Why is the 40 Yard Dash one of the main stats for football? We all know that receivers have to be fast, but the fact is, regardless of which position you play, speed is a vital consideration to college football coaches.

The following is a list of optimal 40 Yard Dash stats that D-I coaches look for in their potential recruits:

Quarterback
- 4.6

Wide Receiver
- 4.5

Running Back
- 4.5

Tight End
- 4.7

Offensive Line
- 5.1

Linebacker
- 4.6

Defensive Line
- 4.8

Defensive Back
- 4.5

Defensive Back (Safety)
- 4.6

Looking at this list, where do you stand? Most likely, there is room for improvement, and the off-season is a perfect time to not only work on conditioning but to also work on speed.

If you are not a natural born speedster, you will need to use a speed-raining program that will improve your speed specifically for football.

Things To Do This Month:
Parents, if your son is beyond is years and already has a good idea about his field of study, you may want to begin thinking about some top schools in the country. For example, is he thinking of a career in science?

Look into some of the Ivy League schools. They do not offer athletic scholarships, but they do have huge endowments and if his grades are impressive enough, he could attend all expenses paid and play football too.

Check the websites of these schools to see what the admittance requirements are. If you think this is way too early to be thinking about a college, think again, today parents are beginning to groom their kids for college from preschool forward.
Continue with off-season conditioning and speed training. Yes, the season is over, but you can use this time to really improve in these areas so you are more than ready for spring training.

Check the schedule for the National Underclassmen Combines tour and try to make plans to attend one in your area. These combines are designed to showcase up and coming freshmen, sophomores and juniors. It is a terrific way to begin getting your name out there.

Chapter 7

FRESHMEN ~ MARCH

Get The Ball Rolling Early

Today, the Internet makes it possible for college football coaches to recruit worldwide. Recruiting profiles, highlight videos and game tapes can be posted on the Web for literally every coach in the country to see instantly. You must think nationally rather than regionally in today's recruiting world; you can no longer just think of being recruited by a school in your state or region.

Parents and athletes, make it your top priority to know and understand the NCAA rules as they apply to football Because of the Internet and social media sites like Facebook, and Twitter, the rules for contacting potential recruits are changing rapidly. Knowing and understanding the rules now will keep you from breaking them and your heart as you move through the recruiting process.

It is important that you get your name in the coach's computer database as early as possible after you have stats. Make it a high priority to contact the schools via email where you might like to

play early on.   See a sample Letter Of Introduction in the
Appendix.

Here's why. Once you appear on their radar, you can update your
information periodically with any accomplishments so the coaches
can track your improvement over you high school football career.

*You and your parents should decide now to be proactive in your
recruiting process.* It could be the difference between receiving a
college athletic scholarship or not. Realize that many coaches
have very limited recruiting budgets and they actually depend on
you to get your information to them.

Once you are in their database, you can send regular updates as to
your accomplishments and improvements. For example, if you
had a 4.8 this year, when you cut it down to 4.6, send them an
update.

*As a freshman football player, you should know what the
'measurables' are for your sport.* As examples, you will be
measured on your vertical jump and bench press and you will be
timed on your 40-yard dash. Remember, these measurables must
be verified in order to count.

*Many high school football players do not realize their dreams of
playing college ball simply because they do know how to honestly
assess their athletic abilities.* They think they are better than they
are and they shoot for unrealistic fits. Start now to be honest about
how fast you are in the 40 and how high you can jump. This will
give you a real evaluation of where you are now and will allow
you to set goals based on the real facts.

Develop Mow-Them-Down Bursts Of Power

Use this time in March to get bigger, faster, and stronger. As
football players you are not only allowed, but you are encouraged
to bulk-up to a certain extent. Too much bulk, though, can lead to
loss of flexibility and speed and can result in injury.

Weight Room Tips:

Use the weights intelligently and correctly. Perform all exercises using full range of motion and good form with no jerking or throwing the weights.

Know how to execute each exercise in your workout program. Using the weights incorrectly can result in injury and will prevent you from obtaining maximum benefits.

Since maximal strength training involves the use of heavy weights to increase explosive bursts of power, it is crucial that you **ALWAYS USE A SPOTTER.**

Realize that only after you have built strength and power in the weight room will you have at your disposal the rock solid muscle foundation to increase your power and strength on the football practice field.

With each rep, visualize yourself moving toward your ultimate goal of landing a College Athletic Scholarship. Doing so will help you keep your goal in sharp focus.

Chapter 8

FRESHMEN – APRIL

Begin To Think Like A College Football Coach
Knowing up front how the coaches at the next level think and what they consider important will go a long way towards making your quest for a college football scholarship a successful one. You want to make it easy for the college football coach to consider you as a potential recruit.

Of course, you must have above average talent, but there are literally tens of thousands of athletes that have good even great talent, how do you turn your talent into the athletic scholarship you are after? Knowing ahead of time what they are looking for will enable you to mold yourself into that standout recruit that is able to catch the coach's eye.

These are a few things that you can begin doing now and continue to do to over your high school career to make sure that you have every chance to be recruited when the time comes:

Train For Good Stats - Make yourself aware of the stats the coaches are looking for at your position, and then do everything in your power during the next few years to either meet or exceed those stats. The coach, depending on his program, receives between 5,000 and 25,000 recruiting packages each year. From these players, he is looking for the ones that have minimum stats to play in his program. Here are the stats of the perfect Division I football player:

Quarter Back
- Height - 6'3"
- Weight - 200
- 40 Yard Dash - 4.6
- Bench - 260
- Squat - 425

Wide Receiver
- Height - 6'2"
- Weight - 185
- 40 Yard Dash - 4.5
- Bench - 235
- Squat - 315

Running Back
- Height - 6'0"
- Weight - 210
- 40 Yard Dash - 4.5
- Bench – 315
- Squat – 415

Tight End
- Height - 6.4
- Weight - 240
- 40 Yard Dash 4.7
- Bench - 300
- Squat - 400

Offensive Line
- Height - 6'4"
- Weight - 280

- 40 Yard Dash - 5.1
- Bench 320
- Squat 450

Linebacker
- Height - 6'1"
- Weight - 220
- 40 Yard Dash - 4.6
- Bench 315
- Squat - 445

Defensive Line
- Height - 6'4"
- Weight - 250
- 40 Yard Dash - 4.8
- Bench - 315
- Squat - 450

Defensive Back
- Height - 6'0"
- Weight - 185
- 40 Yard Dash - 4.5
- Bench – 260
- Squat – 385

Defensive Back (Safety)
- Height 6'2"
- Weight - 200
- 40 Yard Dash - 4.6
- Bench - 270
- Squat - 405

There are exceptions, but if you know what the coaches are looking for, you will be way ahead in your recruiting process. How do you measure up now? Copy these stats and put them where you can refer to them. They give you a goal to shoot for.

Maintain Decent a GPA- Today, academics play a huge role in whether you get recruited or not and they are yet another quick way that coaches eliminate players they are not interested in. Imagine, the coaching assistants sitting down to evaluate five to twenty-five thousand possible recruits, they absolutely must use quick methods to narrow down their pool of potential recruits, and one way is to use a minimum GPA.

Think about it from the coach's point of view, if you won't qualify to be admitted to his institution, why should he bother considering you for his program? **Here are the preferred grades for D-I college football recruits:**
- 3.0 GPA
- ACT score of 24 or higher
- SAT score of 1000 or higher

Keep Your Nose Clean - You are just beginning your high school career, it is really up to you to maintain decent behavior. College coaches are not looking for trouble and will typically pass over a potential recruit that is known for bad behavior.

Contribute To Your Community - recruits that are known in their communities impress Coaches. If you are the type of person that participates in your neighborhood activities, then you may also have the qualities of a leader or good team member. It may sound corny, but the idea is to be a good citizen.

The idea is to make of yourself, as you progress through your high school career, an ideal candidate for the recruiting process. Do well in academics, be an asset to your team, meet the stats for your position, and contribute to your community.
- At this point, you haven't made any mistakes that can't be corrected. Now that you know what college coaches look for, it is up to you to develop the characteristics they are looking for.

Chapter 9

FRESHMEN ~ MAY

Recruiting Dream Team - Do You Have One?
What does the term **'Recruiting Dream Team'** mean and do you
need one?

Your recruiting dream team is composed of you, your parents, or
other interested and involved people that are willing to help you
during all phases of your recruiting process. It could be one or
both of your parents or even one or more of your other family
members. Sometimes grandparents or a big brother can easily
serve in this roll.
Absolutely, *you do NEED a team of people* who are willing to
consistently help you manage your recruiting game plan as you
move through your high school athletic career.

*Getting an athletic scholarship is not an instantaneous one-shot
event*. There are many steps along the way, and help with school
searches, the many letters and emails of introduction, meeting

deadlines, creating athletic profiles and highlight videos, making school visits, and even negotiating with coaches will prove invaluable.

While you can keep up with the recruiting process yourself, it is much easier when you enlist the help and support of at least *one other person who will be committed to your recruiting game plan* efforts. You will be very busy with many activities including practicing and playing football and maybe another sport, your studies, a social life, and your family activities.

Here are just a few of the ways your recruiting dream team can help:

They can *gather college and athletic program information*. They can also write letters or emails of introduction, help with your athletic profile, help create or pay for your highlight videos and they can handle countless other details.

Your dream team *can respond to questionnaires for coaches,* and other requests for information.

Using a filing and tracking system, they can keep coach communication and your whole *recruiting process organized*. This is a huge job, and will become even more important as the different coaches express recruiting interest in you.

When the calls and attention from coaches do begin, your parents or other members of the team can *help you keep your head on straight*. While it is exciting beyond belief, when all the attention starts, if can be overwhelming.

Team members can keep track of your high school academic, extracurricular accomplishments, and athletic achievements, and they can *give timely stats updates to the various coaches.*

Gather together your Recruiting Dream Team now; you will be glad you did. Your parents and other interested family members or even willing friends *can be so much more than a handy secretary.*

You need these people; they can both encourage you and help you keep your feet on the ground when the recruiting process heats up.

What 10th Graders Need To Do

One of our main goals in this book is to educate you about the *real truths of the college football recruiting game*.

That is not always easy as communication technology is constantly improving and changing so rapidly that even the *NCAA is confused and is having trouble keeping up these days.*

As this new technology impacts the way we communicate with each other, coaching contact rules are also changing. While you can still call and receive calls from coaches, *up to 75% of communication between athletes and coaches is carried on via Facebook's inbox and Twitter's instant messaging.*

A very small number (100 – 150 nationwide) of possible football recruits will be actively pursued by college football coaches, the rest of you will have to be proactive in getting yourself a college football scholarship.

What Does Proactive Mean?

Every year a few talented elite or what is commonly referred to as 'blue chip" sophomores will be lucky enough to be actively recruited by the college football coaches, however, the vast majority of you will have to be *PROACTIVE* in your recruiting process. In practical terms, what does proactive mean?

Proactive means that you will have to *MARKET YOURSELF* to the coaches and you and your parents will have to do all the legwork throughout your recruiting process to get them to notice your talents.

Fortunately, this is not all that difficult to do, it you follow a proven set of steps like the ones outlined in this book. The main thing to remember is to do the steps, as they are outlined month by month.

For example, one of the most important things to remember is that regardless of which university you wish to attend, each of them has a minimum GPA requirement. Your GPA is something that accumulates from your freshman though your senior year in high school. If you wait until your final semester in high school to start raising your grade point average, it will, in most cases, be too late. It just makes sense to keep your grades up as you go along.

Chapter 10

SOPHOMORE ~ SEPTEMBER

Eight Things To Do This Month

If you are a standout, this is the year that you can really begin to be taken seriously by the college coaches. Not many of you saw real playing time last year. But this year, your high school coach will probably call you up to see what you can do. If you are serious about playing college football, then you will have to start making every practice and every opportunity to play count from here on in.

Determine to give your best whether it is the weight room or the practice field. No one except you can make an impression on your coach and your fellow teammates. Your team needs an asset, someone that can deliver during the heat of the game. Make of yourself that asset.

1. If you haven't already, **get a recruiting notebook**. Get one that has pockets and start now to keep track of every contact you have with any college coach. Keep track of camp invites, questionnaires, phone calls... Keep track of everything! When things start to heat up recruiting wise, you will be glad you have all this information at your fingertips.

2. **Talk with your parents** about college locations, majors and colleges you are interested in. It is not too early to begin thinking about all of these things. While you may change your mind, it is still good to begin thinking about all the different options that are available to you.

3. Start **gathering information** about and researching colleges academically, socially and athletically. Try to visualize yourself on campus and playing for the schools on your wish list. Also think what it would be like if you were only a student at each of these schools.

4. **Think long-term**! Remember that some coaches are only interested in winning. Your primary focus should be on getting a college education and getting it paid for. Playing football should be secondary to education. For example, think about what you would like to be doing the next 40 years instead of the next couple of years.

5. **Talk about colleges** that would be a good fit for you athletically and academically. Have one or two Div. I dream schools but look at ALL other levels too.

6. **Be Ready!** There is a very good chance that you still haven't seen much playing time yet, but there is also an excellent chance that you could be called up to replace an injured player or just to see how you do in a real game. Make every play and practice session count. If you are perceived as lazy, do you really thing you will be given many chances to play?

7. **Develop a thick skin!** This is the year that your coach is really putting you and your talents to the test to see if he wants to bring

you up next year. Work on any criticism that he gives you and practice to improve in that area.

8. Remember, **stats are accumulating**! Many college coaches like to see improvement from year to year. Try to improve your performance with every game. Very few sophomores have impressive stats; strive to be one of them.

Chapter 11

SOPHOMORE ~ OCTOBER

Things For Sophomores To Begin Thinking About

Keep in mind that **college coaches EXPECT to be contacted by you**, but they do not really want to hear from you until you have significant varsity stats. For the most part, they do not have the recruiting budget to travel around the country and actually see you compete. Instead they use stats, questionnaires, letters or emails of introduction, recruiting profiles, highlight videos and full game tapes (Instructions and samples of all of these can be found in the Appendix at the back of this book).

Obviously, you think you are a collegiate level athlete or you would not have purchased this book, but still it is easy to procrastinate. **Do not wait** until your senior year to begin your college athletic scholarship search. Consider every semester a building block in your athletic scholarship quest.

Do not depend on your high school coach to use his influence to get you admitted into a college. All colleges have minimum academic requirements and poor grades will turn a college coach's attention away from you quicker than a red-hot bullet. When you are researching possible college football programs, note what the minimum academic requirement is and keep your GPA and ACT/SAT scores high enough to be admitted. As we've said, at this point, every single semester counts.

If your grades are less than desirable, it is not too late to adjust your study habits and significantly **improve your grades and scores**.

Speak with **athletes that have already been recruited** at the schools where you would like to play. Ask them about their recruiting process. This will give you a more realistic perspective of how it really works.

Don't think that a football camp invite means that you are being recruited. Because college coaches make a good supplemental income from the camps they put on, they tend to send out these camp invites to every football player in the area. Remember just because you got a camp invite, DOES NOT MEAN YOU ARE BEING RECRUITED, but it could mean that the coach would like to see you play.

Don't believe everything the college coaches tell you during the recruiting process. The truth is that the coaches tend to recruit more potential recruits than they actually have slots for. They over-recruit because they know that not every athlete they talk to will choose their school and they also know that some of the recruits they want will choose other schools.

Before narrowing down the list of schools where you would like to attend, **talk to friends, fans, and your current high school coach about the college football coaches** at different schools. Word tends to get around about a less than honest coach. Also talk with the present athletes on his team.

Chapter 12

SOPHOMORE ~ NOVEMBER

Complying With NCAA Rules

Many recruits and their families are **UNAWARE** of the different ways that the recruiting process can be carried on while still complying with the NCAA rules.

For example, according to the NCAA rules, before September 1st of their Junior year, student athletes *cannot legally receive* more from college coaches than camp invites and questionnaires, nor can the college coaches legally call a recruit before this date.

So how is it that some sophomores and even some freshman claim to have received scholarship offers?

There are basically three main **ways that 'elite' sophomores and freshman do receive offers** before that September 1st date. Remember the *key is that the college coaches cannot contact you* other than to send camp invites and questionnaires, *but you can contact them at your own expense* as much as you want before that September 1st deadline.

This means if a coach **calls you** during your sophomore year, he is in direct violation of the NCAA rule, but if **you call him** no rules have been broken.

This might sound crazy, but if the coach can get word to you in some indirect way that he wants to talk to you **so you will call him**, he is within the rules. He will get someone to act as a relay between the two of you so no NCAA rules are actually broken.

Here Are Three Ways That Sophomores Might Legally Get Scholarship Offers:

1. One way the college coach could get word to you would be to have your high school coach tell you that he wants you for his program. This typically happens when your high school coach has an ongoing relationship with the coach and periodically gives him tips and highlight videos on promising recruits. If the coach has had an opportunity to evaluate you during spring tryouts, you could be offered a scholarship in this manner.

2. Another way the coach could get you to call him is to get one of his past or current players or even a friend of yours to contact you and tell you that the coach would like to hear from you. In this scenario, the coach has good reason to believe that you are scholarship material and has sized you up in some way either through highlight videos or TV clips and may even make an offer to you before some other coach does.

3. Another typical way that sophomore football players get verbal scholarship offers from college coaches before September 1st of their junior year is during summer camps. If you have really

impressed a coach during camp they could verbally make an offer to you before you leave the camp.

If the coach legally verbally offers you like this, the offer should be followed up with a written scholarship offer shortly after September 1st of your junior year.

THINGS TO THINK ABOUT THIS MONTH:

Decide whether to make a **highlight video of your sophomore season**. If you decide to make one, go to the Appendix to see how to make it. Make it as soon as possible after your season ends.

If you do decide to make one after your sophomore season is completely over, there are some important things you should think about.

The higher the quality, the better the college coaches can see your talents. If you are not using a professional service, the same advice holds true; make sure that you get a high quality video regardless of whether you do it yourself, have a friend or your high school coach do it, or hire a professional service.

In most cases, **the coaches will trash a poor quality tape.** Make it easy for the coaches to watch your video and make every frame count.

Here are some tips that will get your video watched provided you have some solid talent:

On the first screen, list your name, your team's uniform color, your jersey number and your position

Include one or two full game tapes at the end of the highlight portion or make a separate DVD for them. Be sure to highlight where you are on the field - use an arrow, draw a circle or square or make a light spotlight around your jersey. The idea is to make it easy for the coaches to identify you in the video.

This may be your only chance to make a good impression, put your best plays in the video early on. Some coaches will only watch the first few clips.

Use ONLY high quality film. No bad lighting or quality issues at all.
Do not include several different clips of one of your hotshot plays.

Before making your highlight video, make sure that you have high quality full game tapes to choose from. If you start with a great full tape, you will get great highlight clips.

Put the DVD in a classy package and do not write on it with an ugly black magic marker.
Make sure all the DVDs work prior to sending them out. Sending out a bad video could easily eliminate you from the competition. The coaches just do not have the time to fool with a bad DVD.

Include your recruiting profile in the package. Although you may have already sent a profile to the coach, having it handy in the package will make it easier for him to review it.

Include your contact information on the DVD including your home phone number, cell phone number, email address, and home address.

Also put your jersey number, height, weight, bench press, 40-time, squat and anything else of major interest that might attract the coach's attention.
There are both pros and cons concerning the value of making a highlight video this early in your high school playing career:

THE PROS ARE:
- *You will be a step ahead of your competition.* If you've had a good varsity season with impressive stats, it is a great time to put yourself on the radar. Make sure the coaches know you are a sophomore and not a junior when you send them the DVD.
- *You will have the video available in case the coach wants to see it and you won't have to scramble around at the last minute.* Making these highlight videos takes time, money and prior preparation.

- **With your hat in the ring early during the recruiting process,** the coach will be able to see your improvement over the course of your high school playing career.

THE CONS ARE:
- Making highlight videos **can get expensive.**
- If you didn't rack up great stats during this season, it **would be a waste of time,** effort and money.
- Many **college coaches don't bother with sophomore videos** unless they are of a blue chip athlete.
- **Early offers, rarely actually materialize from these videos.**

In the final analysis, it is up to you and your parents to decide, however if you were one of the really good solid players who truly had a great season, it probably is a good investment. On the other hand, if you didn't rack up impressive stats, it probably wouldn't pay off other than to give the coaches a base line for comparison purposes.

Chapter 13

SOPHOMORE ~ DECEMBER

Recruiting Dream Teams

What does the term **'Recruiting Dream Team'** refer to and do you need one?
Your recruiting dream team is you and your parents or other interested and involved people that are willing to help you during all phases of your recruiting process. It could be one or both of your parents or even one or more of your other family members. Sometimes grandparents, big brothers or sisters and uncles and aunts can even serve in this roll.

Absolutely, *you do NEED a team of people* who are willing to consistently help you manage your recruiting game plan as you move through your high school athletic career.

Getting an athletic scholarship is not an instantaneous one-shot event. There are many steps along the way, and help with school searches, the many letters and emails of introduction, meeting deadlines, creating athletic profiles and highlight videos, making school visits, and even negotiating with coaches will prove invaluable.

While you can keep up with the recruiting process yourself, it is much easier when you enlist the help and support of at least *one other person who will be committed to your recruiting game plan* efforts. You will be very busy with many activities including practicing and playing football and maybe another sport, your studies, a social life, and your family activities.

Here are just a few of the ways your recruiting dream team can help:

They can *gather college and athletic program information*. They can also write letters or emails of introduction, help with your athletic profile, help create or pay for your highlight videos and they can handle countless other details.

Your dream team *can respond to coach's questionnaires,* and other requests for information.

Using a filing and tracking system, they can keep coach communication and your whole *recruiting process organized*. This is a huge job, and will become even more important as the different coaches express recruiting interest in you.

Your parents or other members of the team can *help you keep your head on straight* when the calls and attention from coaches does begin. While it is exciting beyond belief, when all the attention starts, if can be overwhelming.

Team members can keep track of your high school academic, extracurricular accomplishments, and athletic achievements, and they can *give timely stats updates to the various coaches.*

Gather together your Recruiting Dream Team now; you will be glad you did. Your parents and other interested family members or even willing friends *can be so much more than a handy secretary*. You need these people; they can both encourage you and help you keep your feet on the ground when the recruiting process heats up.
Things To Do In December:

Research NCAA academic requirements and continue striving for academic success. Take a look at the academic requirements of the schools where you are thinking about attending. Make sure that you are on track for all the core requirements for each of these schools as well as the NCAA.

Check with http://www.ncaa.org/ under the Initial Eligibility link for current requirements. NOTE: If math isn't your thing, avoid taking two math classes the same semester. Every final grade you get will count in your overall GPA.

Set up a meeting with your high school counselor and make a list of schools that meet your needs athletically, academically, and socially. As you begin to target schools for your wish list, you can send coaches at those schools a letter or email of introduction expressing your interest in his school. You can find a sample in the Appendix. This initial contact from you to the coaches will establish you in the coaches recruiting computer files as a new athlete to track.
Get a recruiting notebook if you don't already have one. *Keep track of all communications between you and the schools and coaches.* You will be sending updates, follow-up letters and emails, school schedules, and other information to the coaches.

Chapter 14

SOPHOMORE ~ JANUARY

Hit The Weight Room Hard

Developing muscle mass and explosive strength can help make you a desirable football player.

This month, ***use your weight room sessions to continue building muscle mass and overall strength***. These winter months should be used wisely to lay the foundation for your entire resistance-training program. Work hard at the weights now and reap the benefits throughout the next season.

These cold months allow you the opportunity to transform yourself into the kind of powerhouse football player that is known to leave his competition wondering what happened during the off-season.

Your confidence as a player largely comes from knowing that you have given your all in every phase of your training and this includes giving your best to your weight room sessions. Almost no one enjoys sweating at the weights, but it is necessary to your overall recruiting success.

You don't have total control over much in your life, but you do have absolute control over the effort you give in the weight room.

Critical Role Of Parents In The Recruiting Process

Last month, we gave you a quick overview of how *the people on your dream team can assist you with the overwhelming paperwork* involved in the recruiting process.

This month, let's talk about how your parents or other dedicated adult mentors can help you through the process.

They can keep the entire recruiting process in perspective.
Parents should keep mind that a football athlete's career can come to an abrupt end as the result of just one play.

For that reason, academics should be the first consideration for all the schools you have targeted. Your parents, guardian, or other dedicated adults can help you keep your recruiting process in line with this goal.

Your parents or other dream team members *can help you work with your high school coach* during your recruiting process. All of you should realize that your high school coach will be your primary liaison with all the college coaches.

Besides being the all-important hookup with college coaches, *your high school coach can recommend the summer camps* that will be a fit for your particular talents. Exposure in the right camps is an essential part of the recruiting process.

With your college education in mind, your parents can *be very helpful in doing a complete assessment of the colleges on your wish list*. They can evaluate graduation rates, costs, majors, post academic programs campus life, and also athletic programs from a viewpoint that you might not think about. All of this information can be tracked down via the Internet, through your high school counselor's office or by contacting the school directly.

Your parents should be proactive in helping you develop your college wish list and they should go with you on as many preliminary college visits as possible.
When the time comes, *parents should go with you on all official college visits.*

Choosing a college is one of the most important decisions you will ever make. Use the maturity and experience of your parents. They may think of questions and make observations that you would not think of.

The recruiting process is full of ups and downs. *Some coaches will think you are terrific but others may totally reject you.* Your parents can act as a steadying influence through both the highs and lows.

Parents can help you be realistic about your actual football playing abilities. If you are not D-I material, they can help you go for the programs where you will be a fit. Getting a college education and having it paid for should be the ultimate goal.

Your parents and all the other supportive people in your life *should display good sportsmanship* at all your games. There is nothing more embarrassing than having a parent who badmouths you, the other players or the officiating crew.
Things Parents Should Avoid:

They can avoid being an additional stress factor for you. Being supportive without being obnoxious is the idea.

Parents should set their egos aside as they help you select schools where you will be a good fit athletically, academically and socially. The big state university may not suite your athletic talent and other abilities.

Recruiting Things To Do This Month:

Continue sending either emails or letters of introduction to the coaches at the schools where you would like to play. A sample can be found in the Appendix. Doing so will ensure that you are on the radar of these schools.

Continue to work off the field on your athletic skills, physical fitness, and mental toughness. Do a mental check of your character traits. There is still time to improve in every area.

R*egister with the NCAA Eligibility Center if you have not already done so.* Do not leave this for others to do; you are the only one that can register.

Make sure that you are taking the right courses to meet core requirements at the NCAA and also the schools where you are interested in playing.

Develop a filing system for any and everything that has to do with your recruiting process. Paperwork comes in, gets misplaced, discarded or lost. Make a habit of filing all correspondence, catalogs and notes from coaches. You should have a recruiting notebook by now. You will eventually need all this material to help you make your final decision.

Make a point to *talk to other football athletes that have already been recruited.* This can prove invaluable in giving you the inside scoop on how the recruiting process actually works. Also, you might be able to pick up some uniquely helpful tips on certain schools this way.

Chapter 15

SOPHOMORE ~ FEBRUARY

The Perfect D-I Level Player

While sizing up potential recruits for their football programs is not a perfect science, Division I coaches do look for certain optimal stats in their future recruits.

Bear in mind that these are ideal stats for Division I players. There are many exceptions, of course, but the following stats for the various positions courtesy of AthleticScholarships.org will give you some idea of where you stand now and what you should shoot for as your recruiting process moves forward.

Some players will have better stats in some areas and some will have worse, but you can use them as a measuring stick to guide you if you are shooting for a spot on one of the D-I rosters. Do not use these stats to discourage you, but rather to inspire you.

Quarter Back
- Height - 6'3"
- Weight - 200
- 40 Yard Dash - 4.6
- Bench - 260
- Squat - 425

Wide Receiver
- Height - 6'2"
- Weight - 185
- 40 Yard Dash - 4.5
- Bench – 235
- Squat – 315

Running Back
- Height - 6'0"
- Weight - 210
- 40 Yard Dash - 4.5
- Bench - 315
- Squat - 415

Tight End
- Height - 6.4
- Weight - 240
- 40 Yard Dash 4.7
- Bench - 300
- Squat - 400

Offensive Line
- Height - 6'4"
- Weight - 280
- 40 Yard Dash - 5.1
- Bench 320
- Squat 450

Linebacker
- Height - 6'1"
- Weight - 220
- 40 Yard Dash - 4.6
- Bench 315
- Squat – 445

Defensive Line
- Height - 6'4"
- Weight - 250

- 40 Yard Dash - 4.8
- Bench - 315
- Squat - 450

Defensive Back
- Height - 6'0"
- Weight - 185
- 40 Yard Dash - 4.5
- Bench - 260
- Squat - 385

Defensive Back (Safety)
- Height 6'2"
- Weight - 200
- 40 Yard Dash - 4.6
- Bench - 270
- Squat - 405

Preferred Grades for Division I College Football Recruit
- 3.0 GPA
- ACT score of 24 or higher
- SAT score of 1000 or higher

Remember these are guidelines that coaches use to identify very high level recruits. If you fall short in one or two areas, you still may receive recruiting interest from D-I coaches.

Junior Days For Sophomores:
Yes, if you are a standout sophomore player, I mean a really elite one, there is a good possibility that you may be brought on campus for a Junior Day where you will be courted for a possible future position on the team

Junior Days allow you to see the campus and get a real feel for the school and the athletic program. You'll hear from the head coach, view a highlight video of the school, and tour the facilities. If you do get one of these Junior Days invites, attend if at all possible and consider yourself an elite sophomore prospect.

Things To Do This Month:

Continue working on physical fitness and conditioning, use the stats above as your goal.

National Underclassmen combines run from February through July and are a good way for rising freshmen, sophomores and juniors to start getting their names out there for college football programs. Visit National Underclassmen Combines for a schedule of the current year tour.

Continue emailing recruiting coordinators and coaches with your recruiting packet if you have already accumulated some impressive varsity stats.

From the stats above, you can see that it is **extremely important to keep your grades up.** If you have slacked on them so far in high school, you may still have time to bring them up.

Try to visit at least three colleges on your wish list during this year. Family vacations to distant locations are a great way to work in some of these visits.

Chapter 16

SOPHOMORE ~ MARCH

What You Can Do In The Off Season To Get The Jump On The
Recruiting Process
Most of you haven't, as yet, seen much varsity level playing time.
The junior season will be the breakout season for most of you, so
what can you do to really make it the best season possible?

Looking forward to spring practice, what can you do to help your
recruiting chances during the off-season?

If you really are a standout athlete, you may be invited to one or
two Junior Days even though you are a sophomore. *If you are
lucky enough to be invited, do accept.*
Attending one of these events will give you and your parents a
great look at what a college football practice really looks like. As
most players will not be invited until they are actually juniors, it
will also give you a leg up in the recruiting process.

Focus on improving in speed, strength and stamina by visiting the weight room often and making the track your second home. You want to show up at combines, summer camps, and spring practice at the peak of physical condition. Keep picturing in your mind where you want to be physically and measure and note the benchmarks of your success.

Shaving even a tenth of a second off your 40 yd. dash, for example, is substantial as some college coaches use it as a way to eliminate potential athletes from recruiting consideration.

Start selecting summer camps where you want to attend. If would be a good idea to attend one or two at Division I schools so that you can see what your competition looks like. These camps give you a real opportunity to showcase your talents. They also can be great opportunities to pinpoint your weak areas, and besides that, the learning camps are a great way to help you improve as a player.

If you get an invitation, a Nike Combine experience will pit your skills against all the prep players in your area, and like the summer camps, they will also give you a good idea of your athletic and playing ability. It is important to do your best at these combines as they give verifiable measurables (40 yd dash, bench, etc), which must be included on your recruiting profile. You cannot just say you do a 4.6; you must be able to prove it.

Fill out and return all questionnaires from all coaches regardless of the division level. Keep a record of all correspondence from coaches and make a folder in your recruiting notebook for each school. Once you have returned a questionnaire, you will be on that school's radar and you can send update information as to your accomplishments.

The Difference Between Unofficial College Visits and Official College Visits
The difference is mainly in the way the visits are financed. The NCAA as to number of visits and when they can be made governs official visits.

Unofficial visits - are visits where you and your parents pay your own expenses to and from the college; the visits are in no way paid for by the university.

Official visits - are paid for by the university and cannot be taken until the athlete starts his senior year. Most potential recruits take their five allowed official visits after their senior season is over just because they have more time.

Chapter 17

SOPHOMORE ~ APRIL

Picking Summer Camps

Since college football coaches are prohibited from sending anything other than camp invites and questionnaires until Sept 1st of your Junior year, even if you've had some varsity experience, which most of you haven't had, you will not know which if any coaches are actually interested in you at this point. So, what can you do to help your recruiting process when you don't really know where to focus your efforts?

One very important thing that you can do during the upcoming summer is to attend a summer camp or two, but which camp is right for you this early in your high school football career? There are huge advantages to attending good quality summer football camps:

"Summer Camp Advantages..."

You get to see first hand how you measure up against the other players in your area. Attending a Nike camp or one held at a state university will not only bring out the best in you, but you can also get an idea of what the top talent in the region will be like. This is an experience that lets you evaluate your skills in the real world of football recruiting.

The benefits of being coached by college level football coaches at these camps will most certainly elevate your play. You can see for yourself what the teaching and coaching style is at your dream school. Check out how the coaches teach and how they treat the athletes.

Is this program you could play for?
If you have real talent, it will give you an opportunity to show case your playing skills. Word tends to get around about a good prospect. Coaches from other schools will also hear about your talent even if they are not coaching the camp.

It gives you an opportunity to visit your dream school, see the campus, and give you a feel for the area.

Every school that you have contacted will send you an invite to their summer football camp. Coaches send these camp invites out by the thousands. While an invite does mean that you are in their computer base, it does not necessarily mean they are recruiting you.

The bottom line is you can't attend them all, so how do you narrow down your choices?

"Tips For Picking Summer Camps..."
1. Ask the Junior and Senior athletes on your team where they have attended summer camps. A good recommendation from someone is often a good indication of whether the camp is a good one or not.

2. As a sophomore athlete, you should attend a camp that is known to be a teaching camp. You want to attend one that will

help you improve your playing abilities. As we said above, there are many other advantages, but top on the list is that you want to improve you playing skills.

3. Go to the camps with the idea that they will help you become a better player and not to land a football scholarship. Why? While you do hope, of course, that the coaches will notice your talent, your focus, at this point, is to do everything you can to improve your playing abilities. The better football player you are, the better your chances to sign on the dotted line of an athletic scholarship offer when the time comes.

National Underclassmen Combines

Don't forget to attend one of the National Underclassmen Combines, which are held Feb through July across the country. Check for information and to register for the current year events here. Some states only have one combine so check now for the event that is closest to your home.

Contacting College Coaches

If you had a great freshman football season, then you should have contacted the coaches where you would like to play via email so that you could get on their database, if you didn't contact them and you did have great freshman stats, do so now.
Very few of you had that kind of playing time, but looking forward to this coming season, try to do everything you can do to get some great varsity stats so you can write an email introducing yourself to the coaches (sample in the Appendix). When you do contact the coaches, attach your athletic profile (sample and tips in the Appendix).
This introductory email will get you on the radar of the coaches so they can send you questionnaires and camp invites.

Things To Do This Month
Keep up with your academics.

Work on identifying the list of schools that would be a fit for you academically, athletically, and socially. Sit down with your parents and start chatting about where you think you might like to attend. At this point nothing is set in stone, but start thinking about where you would like to attend.

Make use of the weight room as often as you can.

Pay attention during spring practice bearing in mind that how you perform in practice determines how much playing time you will get during this coming season

Chapter 18

SOPHOMORE ~ MAY

Football Combines

Last month we talked about summer camps and how it would be a good idea to attend one or two this summer, but what about the football combines? If you were a standout athlete as a sophomore, you might have received invites to one or more combines.

Should you attend or not?
It is important that you and your parents realize that receiving an invite to a camp or combine does not mean that you are going to get recruited to play football for any school.
The next consideration is price, and price has a lot to do with whether you should attend or not.
Types Of Combines

First, there are free football combines. If you live close to one of these free events like an Under Armour Combine or a Nike Combine, then, by all means, you should attend. Combines are a terrific opportunity for you to pit your skills against other athletes at the event, showcase your talents, and possibly also get some coaching from someone besides your high school coach.

Then there are the National Underclassmen Combines, which cost $89.99 if you pre register and $120.00 if you wait to walk up. If your parents can afford it and you can catch one close to you, then this is also one you could attend. However, keep in mind that attending one of these will not get you recruited, but it will give you the same benefits as the free camps above will do.

Lastly, there are the prestigious combines like the US Army All American Combines that cost a significant amount of money to attend. These combines have no value above the free ones or the National Underclassmen Football Combine discussed above. Besides costing a lot of money, the worst thing is they do NOTHING to help you get recruited. College coaches pay no attention to the results of these expensive combines.

Some of the costly combines brag that the top recruits in the country will be in attendance, but while many top athletes will be there, the fact is that any athlete that can cough up the money will be welcomed to the combine. They are moneymakers for the people that run them and not much more.

So if you can find a free one close to home or you have the $89.99 for a National Underclassmen Combine, then attend with the idea of gaining experience and maybe an opportunity to get coached by someone different, **but do not pay any significant amount of money to attend a combine, and do not attend thinking that it is of any importance as far is getting a scholarship to play football is concerned.**

Chapter 19

SOPHOMORE ~ SUMMER VACATION (Time To Get Ahead)

Camps, Strength, Speed

While it will tempting to loaf this summer, be assured that your competition for college football scholarships are making the most of their summer by increasing speed and building strength. Keep in shape this summer and report to spring training in top form. Your coach and all your team members will appreciate it if you come to practice in great shape.

Attend one or two summer camps if you can. There are enormous benefits to attending summer sports camps as we've discussed above, but one of the more obvious benefits is you will come away from the camp having a realistic evaluation of your skill level and talent as they stack up against the competition.

College Athletic Scholarship puts out separate book on Amazon Kindle called "Sports Camps". It gives you the all the information you need to get the most out of your sports camp experience. You'll learn all about the different types of camps and about which ones would best be suited to meet your particular needs. You'll also learn why paying huge amounts of money for a summer football camp is unnecessary and pretty much a waste of money as far as actually getting you recruited in concerned.

What 11th Graders Need To Do

Your junior year of high school is a very important year as far as being recruited to play college football goes. This is the year that most of you will, for the first time, see extended varsity playing time allowing you to put up impressive stats that will be meaningful to college coaches.

Unfortunately, some student/athletes and their parents still think that if you are good enough to play college football, somehow, magically, the college football coaches will find you. NOTHING could be further from the truth. In the vast number of cases, you will have to be the one to get yourself noticed by the coaches. It will be your proactive marketing efforts that will get that job done.

While there are a few outstanding football players that will almost automatically be recruited, that number is only between 100 – 150 players nationwide. Let me put that number in perspective for you. There are literally thousands of high school athletes that participate in high school football all across the country.

So how do all these other athletes get noticed and land themselves a college football scholarship? They find a proven recruiting program such as the one you are now reading and they stick to that plan. Being recruited to play college football is a simple process composed of only five steps really, but there are many mini steps along the way that make up each step.

The first step is to make a Recruiting Profile composed of your contact information, grades and academic information, honest athletic accomplishments and a picture. Instructions and a sample are in the Appendix of this book.

Next, you and your parents need to work together to find a list of colleges or universities that fit you athletically, socially, and academically. These will become the schools on your wish list.

Learning how to market yourself to the college football coaches is the next step in the recruiting process. Among other things, you will write them an introductory Email telling them of your interest in playing football for their school. Depending on your circumstances, you may also attach your recruiting profile and a link to your highlight video.

Then you will either make or have made a high quality highlight video. This is a very important step in the recruiting process as it shows college coaches what you can do. Most college coaches do not have the funding to travel around the country to actually see potential recruits play so they do depend on seeing good highlight videos.

Initially, you will build a personal athletic website, which will host all your athletic information including accomplishments and your highlight video.

All of these steps are covered and expanded upon within the pages of this book. The Appendix has complete instructions and samples, where needed, on the introductory Email, the recruiting profile, the highlight video and the personal athletic website.

How to complete these five steps and get yourself a few football scholarship offers is what this book is all about. This is the year to really concentrate on doing all the legwork necessary in the recruiting process. There is a lot to do. Enlist the help of your parents and your high school coach if you can.

Chapter 20

JUNIOR ~ SEPTEMBER

September 1st Is A Big Recruiting Day For Juniors

Starting September 1st of your junior year, the coaches can start sending you **'real mail'**, that is mail other than revenue generating camp invites and questionnaires. Both of these are typically sent out by the droves, and are usually meaningless as far as determining whether a coach has any real interest in recruiting you for his team.

Now you can get serious communication from the coaches like hand written notes, game invites, and even scholarship offers if they think you are good enough. These types of communication from the coaches show genuine interest in you. If you do have a written scholarship offer at this time, consider yourself among the very lucky few.

The facts are, though, that most of you will have to wait until later to receive scholarship offers, but there are a number of important things you can do this month to move yourself up to the top 2% of all the high school football players in the country.

You should **be on the radar of all the schools** where there is even a remote chance you will eventually play. That is you should have sent a letter of introduction and your recruiting profile to all the football programs at schools where you have dreamed about playing, those where you wouldn't mind playing and also to some other ones where you are a **sure fit** both academically and athletically.

Recruiting Activity Should Be Speeding Up

Now that you are a junior, **recruiting, for you, should be speeding up**. We're not saying that the signing day fireworks should start, but, by now, you and your parents should be well on your way to marketing you and your talent to college football coaches.

What does the term marketing mean?

If you have achieved significant varsity statistics this past year, here is the minimum marketing you should have done:

A Letter of Introduction or an Email introducing yourself should have been sent to all the coaches where you have an interest in playing

Your Recruiting Profile should be attached to your letter of introduction or initial contact

Email and sent to these same coaches

You should have a personal athletic website up and running.

And you and your parents should be seriously thinking about how you will get your highlight video done after this season ends.

If no marketing has been done, it is definitely time to get cracking. Use this time and the Appendix in this book to develop your:

- Letter of introduction or initial contact Email,
- Recruiting profile,
- Athletic website
- Highlight video.

Letter of Introduction

In most cases, your **Letter of Introduction** or initial contact email should be sent to the recruiting coordinator (go to the college websites and look him up in the staff directory of the athletic site). If you already know and have worked with a specific position coach during college football camps in the past, send the contact email to him.

Go to the Appendix to see a sample. Here are some things to consider as your write this short and simple first communication to the coaches.

- It should be written by you with your parents guidance and be grammatically correct with correct spelling.
- Be short and to the point
- Tell a little bit about yourself (where and what year you play) that you have researched schools and the coach's school is where you would like to play. Do not sent the same mass email to all the coaches. Make it relevant to their school.

If you have already built a recruiting profile, attach it as a .pdf , .doc or .xls to your email or print it out and put it in with the letter.

Recruiting Profile

Briefly, here is what should be included in your **Recruiting Profile**. Go to the Appendix to see a sample:

- **Your Contact Information** including home phone, cell phone, email address both yours and your parents and home address. If possible, get permission from you high school coach about including his email too.

- **Grades and Academic Information** including grade point average and any ACT or SAT scores you have, and class rank if you can get it from your guidance counselor.
- **Athletic Accomplishments** including honest stats that you and your team have achieved.
- **Include A Picture of Yourself** with a pleasant expression so the coaches can recognize you when recruiting gets serious.

Put it in either .pdf, .doc. or .xls. Most coaches can open these.

Personal Athletic Website

Your **personal website** is primarily to give the coaches a quick way to find out about your stats, your talent and your accomplishments and it gives them easy access to your highlight videos. This website is strictly for the convenience of the coaches. Many of you will know how to put up a web page, others will need to depend on techy friends and some will have to hire it done. Whichever route you take, here some things to consider:

- The **domain name should be your own name**, for example if your name is Thomas Webster, register a domain as www.thomaswebster.com, but if that is taken register as www.thomaswebster44 (your jersey number) or websterfootball.com, or your name and your birth year.
- Remember, we said **your personal website was for the convenience of the coaches**. You can email the link to the coaches or you can tell the coaches to go to your personal website. Registering the domain with your name and jersey number is a great way to get him to remember you and your number.
- **Having your video online is a quick and cheap way to get your information reviewed by coaches**. Coaches can click a link and see your stats and highlight video within just seconds.
- Basically the information including your picture that you put in your profile should be posted on your website, and

you should regularly update it with new stats and accomplishments.

- **DO NOT PUT PERSONAL COMMENTS ON THIS WEBSITE**
- **Post your highlight videos** on your website.

Chapter 21

JUNIOR ~ OCTOBER

Apply To All Level Schools

If you even **suspect that you may not be a good fit for the D-1** programs in your state or around the country, then you should also send your recruiting profile as outlined to those lower level D-1AA, D-11, and even D-111 schools where you know you would be a fit. Also, fill out and return every single questionnaire from every school that sends you one. This is an efficient way to, at least, get on their recruiting radar if you aren't already.

Make Sure To Apply Where You Are A Good Fit

Remember, it is far better to get to **play the sport you love in college** and get your college paid for than it is to hold out for a powerhouse football program that may be showing only mild interest in you. Make sure that you have applied to enough schools where you KNOW you will be a fit.

These football scholarships can easily be **worth a hundred thousand dollars** and many are worth twice that figure. Leaving college with a degree that equips you to make it in the world and with no debt to boot is something that few college graduates today can claim.

Are You Registered With The NCAA?

If you have not already **registered with** the NCAA Eligibility Center, use this link to do so now. This is the official site, which determines each high school athlete's eligibility to participate in college sports, and it is the authority on your high school academic credentials.

Complying With NCAA Rules

Many recruits and their families are **UNAWARE** of the different ways the recruiting process can be carried on while still complying with the NCAA rules.

For example, according to the NCAA rules, before September 1st of their Junior year, student athletes *cannot legally receive* more from college coaches than camp invites and questionnaires, nor can the college coaches legally call a recruit before this date.

Due to social media like Facebook and Twitter, the NCAA rules regarding how college coaches can contact potential recruits has seen changes recently. Make it your business to know the current rules so that you are always in compliance.

THINGS TO THINK ABOUT THIS MONTH

Decide whether to make a **highlight video of your sophomore season**. If you decide to make one, go to the Appendix to see how to make it.

If you do decide to make one, there are some important things you should think about.

The higher the quality, the better the college coaches can see your talents. If you are not using a professional service, the same advice holds true; make sure that you get a high quality video regardless of whether you do it yourself, have a friend or your high school coach do it, or hire a professional service.

In most cases, **poor quality tapes will be trashed by the coaches.** Make it easy for the coaches to watch your video and make every frame count.

Here are some tips that will get your video watched provided you have some solid talent:
On the first screen, list your name, your team's uniform color, your jersey number and your position

Include one or two full game tapes at the end of the highlight portion or make a separate DVD for them. Be sure to highlight where you are on the field - use an arrow, draw a circle or square or make a light spotlight around your jersey. The idea is to make it easy for the coaches to identify you in the video.

This may be your only chance to make a good impression, put your best plays in the video early on. Some coaches will only watch the first few clips.
Use ONLY high quality film. No bad lighting or quality issues at all.

Do not include several different clips of one of your hotshot plays. Before making your highlight video, make sure that you have high quality full game tapes to choose from. If you start with a great full tape, you will get great highlight clips.
Put the DVD in a classy package and do not write on it with an ugly black magic marker.

Make sure all the DVDs work prior to sending them out. Sending out a bad video could easily eliminate you from the competition. The coaches just do not have the time to fool with a bad DVD.

Include your recruiting profile in the package. Although you may have already sent a profile to the coach, having it handy in the package will make it easier for him to review it.

Include your contact information on the DVD including your home phone number, cell phone number, email address and home address.

Also put your jersey number, height, weight, bench press, 40-time, squat and anything else of major interest that might attract the coach's attention.

Chapter 22

JUNIOR ~ NOVEMBER

Think Like A College Coach

This is very likely your big year, the time for you to really capture the spotlight as far as the recruiting process goes. If you didn't get much playing time as a sophomore, as the seniors move on, you will probably move up to play.

Learning how to think like a college football coach will do more to help you plan a successful recruiting campaign than almost anything else you could do. Why? Understanding his motives, his time frames, his enormous pressures will help you plan a recruiting campaign that can help him choose you as a recruit.

You must develop the ability to get him to notice and want you for his program in an efficient manner that fits into the recruiting practices and patterns that he has already established. Provided you have above average talent, here are a few pointers that will help establish you as a top contender on the football programs you are shooting for:

Get On His Radar - If you haven't already, either you or your parents should send an introductory email to all the coaches where you have an interest in playing. The purpose of this email is to establish you in the coach's database of potential recruits.

This email should be ***brief*** and should include an attachment of your recruiting profile, link to your highlight video if you have one and also a link to your personal website. This is not the time for parents to write a sales letter about your wonderful accomplishments.

You will probably hear back from several coaches thanking you for your interest and inviting you to their football camps. The coaches use these camps to make extra money and they send out thousands of camp invites. They also use them to help evaluate potential players, but mostly they are moneymakers for their programs. As a general rule, don't put much stock in a camp invite.

Push For Great Stats - Make yourself aware of the stats the coaches are looking for at your position, and do everything in your power to either meet or exceed those stats. The coach, depending on his program, receives between 5,000 and 25,000 recruiting packages like yours.

He doesn't have time to slowly plow through every recruiting profile, so he typically scans the front page of your recruiting profile where your stats should be prominently displayed. He uses your stats as an eliminator to help him weed through all those profiles quickly.

While you and you parents may have spent hours creating the profile, you will be lucky if he gives it 30 seconds, and this is why it is so important for you to have minimum stats. Following are the stats of a perfect D-I Level player:

Quarter Back

- Height - 6'3"
- Weight - 200
- 40 Yard Dash - 4.6
- Bench - 260
- Squat - 425

Wide Receiver
- Height - 6'2"
- Weight - 185
- 40 Yard Dash - 4.5
- Bench - 235
- Squat - 315

Running Back
- Height - 6'0"
- Weight - 210
- 40 Yard Dash - 4.5
- Bench – 315
- Squat – 415

Tight End
- Height - 6.4
- Weight - 240
- 40 Yard Dash 4.7
- Bench - 300
- Squat - 400

Offensive Line
- Height - 6'4"
- Weight - 280
- 40 Yard Dash - 5.1
- Bench 320
- Squat 450

Linebacker
- Height - 6'1"
- Weight - 220
- 40 Yard Dash - 4.6
- Bench 315
- Squat - 445

Defensive Line
- Height - 6'4"
- Weight - 250
- 40 Yard Dash - 4.8

- Bench - 315
- Squat - 450

Defensive Back
- Height - 6'0"
- Weight - 185
- 40 Yard Dash - 4.5
- Bench – 260
- Squat – 385

Defensive Back (Safety)
- Height 6'2"
- Weight - 200
- 40 Yard Dash - 4.6
- Bench - 270
- Squat - 405

Of course, there are exceptions, but if you know what the coaches are looking for, you will be way ahead in your recruiting process.

Maintain Decent GPA and SAT/ACT scores -Today, academics play a huge role in whether you get recruited or not and they are yet another quick way that coaches eliminate players they are not interested in. Imagine the coaching assistants sitting down to evaluate five to twenty-five thousand potential recruits; they absolutely use these quick ways to pick their top recruits.
Think about it from the coach's point of view, if you won't qualify to be admitted to his institution, why should he bother considering you for his program? **Here are the preferred grades for D-I college football recruits:**
- 3.0 GPA
- ACT score of 24 or higher
- SAT score of 1000 or higher

Keep Up With All Communication Between You & Coaches -You should have a recruiting notebook by now where you track everything - notes, phone calls, texts, emails - EVERYTHING. Tracking like this will help you and each coach remember what has been said.

Remember, you are one person who is the most familiar with your situation, but he has many hopefuls that he is dealing with. Being able to trigger his memory about you and what has been said or communicated between you will make his job easier

Chapter 23

JUNIOR ~ DECEMBER

Questions For College Coaches

December sees most football coaches concluding their regular seasons with time now to hit the phones. Hopefully, you will start receiving calls from the schools on your wish list (your dream schools) and from some of the coaches at your backup schools too. It is important that you ***think ahead about what you are going to talk about with the coaches*** when they call. This will let them know that you are aware of the recruiting process and that you have thought about what you hope to gain from your college experience.

A good way to do this is to ***formulate a list of questions that*** you will ask each coach when he calls. Keep the list of questions with you either on paper or on your phone. Be sure to jot down notes about the answers and enter them in your recruiting notebook.

Here are a few questions to choose from. You may use all or just part of them as they apply to you:

How would you describe your coaching style? Coaching styles do vary and you want to find out if you can learn and play under his motivation and discipline style.

Describe how you see my roll on the team. By the time the coach calls you, he probably already has a pretty good idea about how you will fit into his overall strategy.

What are your realistic expectations for the team this coming year? Of course, he will say he wants to win, but realistically what is he hoping

What kind of time and physical expectations are involved for team members? College academics are more difficult; you will need to know how much time you will have to complete your studies.

What is your position on academics? Coaches vary on their philosophy on academics. You need to know what his position is. In fact, this is so important, that you need to find out from his current players.

What percentage of your players actually graduate in four years? The NCAA has recently increased its cut line from 900 to 930, which means a higher percentage of athletes must graduate. Remember, while it is exciting to get calls from coaches, your main objective should be to get your college education.

Describe your scholarship program and tell me how your walk-on system works. Both will vary from school to school.

Will my major allow plenty of time for practice and playing football? Many majors have labs and additional outside class hours. Make sure that you will have time to complete your class work.

What is typical day like for a new recruit? He should give you a typical schedule including practice and game times, study, meals, and academics. This information can help you decide if his program will allow you to complete your major.

What is the average class size at your school? Some schools use teaching assistants for large classes. His answer will tell you how much attention you will be getting from professors.

Are there tutors for team members? This information will let you know what help you can expect from the school.

Tell me about the dorm or housing situation at your school and is housing included in the scholarship? This is key information that could determine whether you commit to his school or not.

Is the scholarship you are offering me a full-ride or just a partial? Get him to tell you exactly what his scholarship offer covers. *If his scholarship offer doesn't cover all expenses, is there other financial aid available from his school?* It is important that you know how much out-of-pocket money, if any, your family will have to come up with.

Does my scholarship offer cover summer expenses? Many football players take only a minimum number of credits during the school year and must take some classes during the summer.

What happens to my scholarship if I get injured and can't play? The NCAA has recently voted to allow schools to offer four-year scholarships. Previously, scholarships were extended one year at a time. Each conference has to vote on the proposal, so make sure that your offer is for four years.

Can I work while receiving a scholarship? What is the policy for athletes working during the football season and during summer vacations?

Things To Do This Month

Make sure that your dream team (you, your parents and or other persons that have committed to help you with your recruiting process) *has done the things to market you to all the schools on your wish list*. This list should include schools from every division level.

By now, the schools should have received letters or emails of introduction with your athletic profile attached and you should have your personal website up. *Develop templates for the profile and letter or email of introduction and fit it to each new school.* See Appendix for samples.

If you haven't already, finalize your highlight video from this season making sure to start with only quality videos. See the Appendix for video dos and don'ts. Remember to post the highlight video on your personal athletic website.

After your season is finished, update your recruiting profile to include stats from this season. Be sure to update your personal website and also your Facebook and Twitter accounts.

After your final game, follow up with an email to the coaches you have already contacted to make sure they got your marketing information, to forward your updated recruiting profile, to alert them to any outstanding accomplishments, and to tell them you have a highlight tape available for them to see.

When thinking about the top four or five schools on your target list, make sure that your GPA and test scores are on target to meet the minimum requirements for admission. If not, there is still time to buckle down raise them.

Chapter 24

JUNIOR ~ JANUARY

Six Key Ways College Coaches Find Football Players

As we said above, your name, face, and talents must be brought to the attention of the coaches. ***You've got to get your name in the coaches' computer database of prospective athletes.*** It is a known fact that some coaches start out with a database of 5000 – 25,000 student/athletes and then begin narrowing the list down as they get more information about and from prospects and see them play.

So, let's look at the six primary ways that college coaches find athletes for their football teams:

After you are established in the coach's database, you will be on his radar and when he needs to fill a particular position, *he will look at people in his database first*.

This may seem like a no-brainer, but you need to *establish and maintain a good relationship with your high school coach*. This person could be an important asset to you in your recruiting process. Prove to him that you are of excellent character in addition to being a terrific athlete.

Being named All State either your sophomore or junior year is a great advantage. College coaches have their assistants surf the net checking these lists for promising recruits. Even if you have not sent your information to these coaches, this is enough to put you on their radar.

Attending various *football camps and combines* can get you on their radars too. Coaches obtain the published results of the combines and the Nike camps are free. These are also excellent ways to meet college coaches and for them to see you play.

Sites like Rivals.com and others like it are today great tools for the college football coaches. They regularly check these sites for talent to play for their programs.

Paid recruiting and scouting services. Some of these services send out hundreds of names to the coaches, which tends to reduce their value; however, there are some legitimate paid services that do work hard to get you recruited.
Keep in mind though, before you and your parents break the bank to hire one of these expensive services, your own proactive self-promotion can accomplish pretty much the same thing.

Other Things To Do This Month

Visit some campuses where you are interested in attending.
Make the most of these visits by talking with athletes, students that are not athletes, and professors in your major field if you already have one. Eat in the campus cafeteria at each school and ask the other students about dorm life. Visit both large and small campuses and ask yourself where you feel more at home.

Have You Started Marketing Yet?

As a junior, you marketing campaign to the college coaches where you would like to play should be well underway. Do not delay; make sure that all schools on your list have your introductory email, recruiting profile, highlight video, and a link to your personal athletic website.

Chapter 25

JUNIOR ~ FEBRUARY

Signing Day Is Only Twelve Months Away

As you know, signing day is always in early February, which means that college football coaches are very busy during the first few days of the month, but the good news is that you still have an entire year to do all the things necessary to land yourself either a full-ride football scholarship or at least one of a substantial size.

Recruiting Profile

Hopefully many of you have already done this, but if you haven't, during this important month, you and your parents should make sure that you have put together a *Recruiting Profile,* which should include the following information:

Contact Information - You cannot send the coach too many ways to get in touch with you. Include your name, address, home and cell numbers and also email address. Also send your parents contact information and if you have asked permission, include your high school coach's contact information.

Academics and Grades - First, be honest when reporting this type of information. The better your grades and test scores, the more opportunities you will have to play. Unless you are going for one of the Ivy league schools, a 3.3 GPA and a 23 ACT is all you will need to meet the entrance requirements for most other schools. If you know it or can get it, also furnish your class rank.

Your Picture - A smiling photo will acquaint the coaches with you even before they actually meet you.

Athletic Accomplishments - Include the usual stats, but also include things like team records, postseason honors, and team accomplishments, and also include the same type of information if you have played more than one sport. Again, be truthful with all this type of information.

See the Appendix for a sample and profile layout instructions.

Once you've completed the profile, **send it in a .pdf or .doc file** to everyone you can think of besides the college coaches just to see if there are issues opening it and to get your family and friends to review it for grammar and typos.

Where To Send Your Recruiting Profile

Do you already have a list of schools where you would like to play? Have you and your parents researched schools that would actually be a fit athletically and academically? What type of college program would realistically suit you? Here's how to develop a list of colleges where you would be a fit.

Have a big family meeting where everyone is comfortable putting in his two cents worth. Come at it from a number of different angles with people who know you best:

- **Academics** - Think about what fields of interest you have. What are you good at academically? Do you already know your major? What career do you imagine for yourself? Remember, college is preparation for where you will be spending about forty years of your life.
- **School Size** - Have you imagined yourself attending a school with a student body of forty thousand or more or would you be more at home in a smaller school, say five thousand or less?
- **Location Of School** - Would you be comfortable living clear across the country from your family, or would closer to home suit your personality better? Remember, it is more expensive to travel back and forth from long distances than it is from the in-state schools.
- **Athletics** - Time to get really honest on this one. What level of college football can you realistically play? Ask yourself, your high school coach and your parents. Hopefully, they will all agree, but ultimately you must decide. If you know now that you are not D-I material, shoot for a level of play where you feel you would realistically be a fit.
- **Finances** - Obviously, you are hoping to land an athletic scholarship, but you should also be striving for other types of scholarships as well. It is very possible that you will be offered a partial football scholarship and the rest of the money will have to come from somewhere else. Are you parents willing and able to foot the rest of the bill?

Once you and you parents and other interested family members have talked about these issues, then it is time to start researching schools where you will be a good fit all the way around.

Try to find 25 to 40 schools that meet the criteria derived from your family discussion above. Even if you are pretty sure you are D-I material, select schools from all the other levels. This may prove to be very beneficial to you as signing day twelve months from now moves closer.

How To Send Profile

Now, send your profile to these schools. Go to our College Coaches Online section and find the schools on your list. Just click on the school, under the athletics department, click on the staff directory.

This will give you a list of all the coaches, if you can find the position coach listed, send your introductory email to him (see Appendix for sample), **attach your recruiting profile with a link to your highlight video and personal athletic website** if you have them.

If you do not know the position coach, send everything to the recruiting coordinator. *DO NOT SEND it to the head coach*, he has his staff do all the sifting through the many hundreds and sometimes thousands of profiles for potential scholarship recipients.

Parents, you will probably be handling this for your son. Write the email from you (do not pretend it is from your son) saying a few things about your son's highest accomplishments, link to the video and website, attach the recruiting profile and thank the coach for considering your son. Avoid being long winded about your son's accomplishments and be honest.

You should at least get several camp invites as a result of this email, **if you do not hear from some of the coaches within a couple of weeks, resend your information.** Camp invites do not mean that you are being recruited, but do; at least, mean that you are on the recruiting radar.

Junior Days

Some Coaches hold Junior Days during this month. At a Junior Day you will hear from the head coach, get a fee meal, tour the facilities, listen to the head coach and other coaches pitch the school and football program, view a short school highlight video, and you may have a coach's position meeting.

In addition, you will hear talks about the importance of maintaining a good GPA, coaches will encourage you to attend their summer camp, and they will tell you to keep up the good work and be patient about receiving a scholarship.

A Junior Day invite can come anytime between January and May.

"Things To Do This Month..."

· If you have not already done so, complete your recruiting profile, highlight video and get your athletic website up.

· Send the package as above to the schools on your list. Research schools and come up with a good list of 25 to 40 schools.

· Make Junior Day visits only to schools on the top of your list, but do visit ones where you will be a fit.

Chapter 26

JUNIOR ~ MARCH

Obtain Support Of Your High School Coach

Obviously, you have decided to play football in college and you are reading this so you will know how to get your self recruited and win a college athletic scholarship, so now you are methodically doing all the things necessary to accomplish those goals.

One of the important things you must do it get your high school coach on your side.

Hopefully, you already have a great relationship with your current football coach, but if not, March would be a terrific time to have a real open conversation with him about your dreams of playing football at the next level. While you do need the support of your parents, his support is right up there in importance next to your parents.

Here are some tips to help you obtain his support:

· Make an appointment with him to discuss your desire to play collegiate level football and to find out what he knows about the college athletic recruiting process.

· Ideally, he already knows some of the college coaches in your area and perhaps he has previously seen some of his players get signed. At any rate, this meeting will get the wheels turning in his head about where you might possibly be a fit. College coaches may come calling in April and May, and you want to be upper most in his mind.

· Since your high school coach knows your playing ability probably better than anyone, just point blank ask him what Division level he thinks would be a fit for you. While his opinion of your playing ability is not the be-all-end-all, it should weigh heavily on the college programs that are on your dream list.

· Once your high school coach knows about your desire to play college level football, he will be more apt to help you get ready for the important upcoming summer camps, and with getting you invited to those camps.

If you have already got all your marketing done, that is if you have researched colleges and developed a list of schools, contacted the college coaches by email or letter expressing your interest in playing football at those schools, sent out your recruiting package and made your highlight video, then you are up-to-date with your recruiting process and now have time to focus on getting ready for the next round of summer camps. If you don't have all your marketing done, visit the Appendix for samples and instructions on the above.

Getting Ready For Summer Camps

This month gives you time to focus on and improve your athletic abilities so that you can really shine at the upcoming summer camps and gain the attention of some college football coaches. Hit the weights and the track and get yourself in top physical condition for these camps and focus on the following:

1. 40 Yard Dash
2. Shuttle run
3. Vertical Jump
4. One on ones

Many of you have already attended a camp or two last year and you will know what happens and what the coaches expect. You are ahead of the game because you have the opportunity this month to train hard in the areas where you were weak last year.

Do not underestimate the importance of the summer camps; they are an opportunity for you to be seen by college coaches and scouts.

Keep Up With All Communication Between You & Coaches - You should have a recruiting notebook by now where you track everything - notes, phone calls, texts, emails - EVERYTHING. Tracking like this will help you and the coach remember what has been said.

Remember, you are the person who is the most familiar with your situation, but he has many hopefuls that he is dealing with. Being able to trigger his memory about you and what has been said or communicated between you will make his job easier

Chapter 27

JUNIOR ~ APRIL

Expect Visits From College Coaches This Month
Spring Evaluation, April 15 until May 31, is a time when college
recruiting coaches can legally pay a visit to your high school to
either evaluate your football talent, your academics or both. They
will be looking at your transcripts, talking to your coach, and they
will also be sizing you up face-to-face in what is called the 'eyeball
test'.

According to NCAA rules, the recruiting coaches are not supposed
to do more than say hello to you if they should run into you in the
halls of your high school, but the main thing is they want to see if
you measure up in person to the weight and height you have listed
on your profile. This entire 'hello' meeting makes up the 'eyeball
test'. Make sure that you have been honest about what is on your
recruiting profile.

Here are some tips to help you measure up during the eyeball test:

- *Wear your BIG shoes* - Wear the shoes that make you look the tallest. Ask your parents or your girlfriend which shoes make you look the tallest. This may sound comical, but if you have put down that you are 6'3" and wear flip-flops, you may appear shorter than your stated height.
- *Straighten Up During The Eyeball* - Obviously, slouching makes you appear shorter. You want them to be aware of your full height.
- *Wear The Right Clothes* - If you have been hitting the weight room, you will want to wear a tight T-shirt to show off your bulked up muscles. If you have lost weight since your season ended, wear loose clothing to hide that you've lost the weight.
- *Appear Confident* - The best way to appear that you have self-confidence is to look the recruiting coaches in the eye when you are saying hello.

Coaches Can Call You Now

During spring evaluation period (April 15 until May 15), coaches can make one call per athlete. You may receive one or several of these calls from various coaches. Be prepared to receive the calls from them, as they are a clear indication that the coach is interested in recruiting you.

NOTE: The coach can make one call to you where he actually either talks to you or leaves a message. If he doesn't get you and doesn't choose to leave a message, it doesn't count as his one call. If you see on your display, that he has called you without leaving a message, you can call him back and that also does not count toward his one call. You can call him as many times as you wish.

Here are some tips to make the most of your call from the coaches:

- *Turn off all distractions* including video games, TV and anything else that could take your attention away from the call.

- *Ask the coach questions* - Doing so will show him that you know something about his program and you are really interested in the possibility of playing for him. Print out a list of questions beforehand that you can have ready. You could ask things like: where do you see your program going in the next few years? Do you think you and your staff will be there for the next few years? What is the training staff like at your school? Are tutors available? What did you think of my highlight video? Who is in front of me at my position? There are many more, and this is the time to ask the questions that concern you. Check Chapter 4 for a more complete list of possible questions to ask the coaches.

During April, you could make some visits to colleges to watch spring practices and games. Observe the team, but especially watch the athlete playing at your position, and also watch the coaches and their style. Is it all something you could live with?

Things To Do This Month:
Focus on improving in speed, strength and stamina by visiting the weight room often and making the track your second home. You want to show up at combines, summer camps, and spring practice at the peak of physical condition. Keep picturing in your mind where you want to be physically and measure and note the benchmarks of your success.

Shaving even a tenth of a second off your 40 yd. dash, for example, is substantial as some college coaches use it as a way to eliminate potential athletes from recruiting consideration.

Start selecting summer camps where you want to attend
It would be a good idea to attend one or two at Division I schools so that you can see what your competition looks like. These camps give you a real opportunity to showcase your talents. They also can be great opportunities to pinpoint your weak areas, and besides that, the learning camps are a great way to help you improve as a player.

If you get an invitation, a Nike Combine experience will pit your skills against all the prep players in your area, and like the summer camps, they will also give you a good idea of your athletic and playing ability. It is important to do your best at these combines as they give verifiable measurables (40 yd dash, bench, etc), which must be included on your recruiting profile. You cannot just say you do a 4.6; you must be able to prove it. One very important thing that you can do during the upcoming summer is to attend a summer camp or two, but which camp is right for you this early in your high school football career? There are huge advantages to attending good quality summer football camps:

"Summer Camp Advantages..."
You get to see first hand how you measure up against the other players in your area. Attending a Nike camp or one held at a state university will not only bring out the best in you, but you can also get an idea of what the top talent in the region will be like. This is an experience that lets you evaluate your skills in the real world of football recruiting.

The benefits of being coached by college level football coaches at these camps will most certainly elevate your play. You can see for yourself what the teaching and coaching style is at your dream school. Check out how the coaches teach and how they treat the athletes.

Is this a program you could play for?

If you have real talent, it will give you an opportunity to showcase your playing skills. Word tends to get around about a good prospect. Coaches from other schools will also hear about your talent even if they are not coaching the camp.

"Tips For Picking Summer Camps..."
1. Ask the senior athletes on your team where they have attended summer camps. A good recommendation from someone is often a good indication of whether the camp is a good one or not.

2. As a junior athlete, you should attend a camp that is known to be a teaching camp. You want to attend one that will help you improve your playing abilities. As we said above, there are many other advantages, but top on the list is that you want to improve your playing skills.

3. Go to the camps with the idea that they will help you become a better player and not to land a football scholarship. Why? While you do hope, of course, that the coaches will notice your talent, your focus, at this point, is to do everything you can to improve your playing abilities. The better football player you are, the better your chances to sign on the dotted line of an athletic scholarship offer when the time comes.

Chapter 28

JUNIOR ~ MAY

Spring Evaluation Period - What Does A Call From A College Football Coach Mean?

The spring evaluation period runs from April 15th through May 31, and as a Junior, you or your parents or other interested relative can get ONE call from a head coach or his coaching staff. But what exactly does one of these spring evaluation calls mean?
As we have said before, it means the school is definitely interested in you as a potential prospect, but it does not necessarily mean that you are their top prospect for a certain position. Having said that, if you are a top national prospect, you can be fairly certain that the call means they want you for their program.

On average, a school will place calls to around one hundred and fifty prospects during the spring evaluation period.

Some of the calls will go to A list prospects, these are the prospects that all the other football programs are hoping to sign too. These will be their top picks.

Another group of calls will go to their B list, these are the prospects that they are less serious about and may still want to see face-to-face in the famous 'eyeball' test, and they may want them to also attend their summer camp.

Lastly, there will be calls going out to their C list of potential recruits. These are the recruits that are liked by the coaches, but so far these recruits, as of yet, haven't received any attention from other schools. The coaches could be waiting until another school makes an offer before they get too serious about the recruit.

So as you can see, the spring evaluation calls could mean everything from they really want you for their program to almost nothing. But at the very least, a call means they are interested in you to some degree. You have no way of knowing how far up the leader board you are just from getting one of these calls.

Avoid letting one of these calls throw you off track in your recruiting process, it is a long way from an evaluation call to signing day on Feb. 1st of your Senior year.

If you have received a call from a school on your wish list, you can be cautiously optimistic, but to be safe, continue to recruit many different schools at all levels.

Chapter 29

JUNIOR ~ SUMMER VACATION

Strength, Speed, Summer Football Camps

If you are serious about winning a college football scholarship, then make use of your summer vacation. Continue to work on physical fitness, conditioning and speed.

Take this time to attend at least one or two summer camps. Make sure that you attend a camp hosted by the school that is on the top of your wish list. This will give you an opportunity to see the coaching staff in action.

National Underclassmen combines run from February through July and are a good way for rising freshmen, sophomores and juniors to start getting their names out there for college football programs. Visit National Underclassmen Combines for a schedule of the current year tour.

What 12th Graders Need To Do

If you desire to play college football and you are also hoping to land a college athletic scholarship, you only have a few months left to convince the college football coaches that you are good enough to be signed for their teams on a football scholarship.

Signing day is always in early February, usually on the first Wednesday of the month, so while it is still entirely possible for you to be recruited, you should know that many student/football players in the ninth, tenth, and eleventh grades all across the country and really the world have also been diligently working hard to market themselves, and basically they are ahead of you in the game. Having said that, if you have real football talent, you can still end up signing on the dotted line for a college football scholarship. It is done all the time. You will just have to work harder and faster.

For those of you that have just now started to shine as football players, you and your parents will have to work doubly hard to stay on top of your recruiting process between now and early February. Many seniors have already been offered scholarships, and to them we say congratulations, but what about the ones that really want to play football at the next level, but haven't yet, as seniors, received any real interest from college football recruiting programs?

This book on senior football recruiting will help you quickly move through the recruiting process so you can get official visit invites and football scholarship offers before signing day hits a few months from now.

The talk and excitement around your high school this year will be focused on football scholarships. While it is important to step-by-step complete the recruiting process as outlined in this book, it is equally important to keep your mind on your own football season. This is your last chance to improve your position in the race for the football scholarship you have been dreaming about.

Before we go in further, you and your parents should be completing plans for your midseason and end of season highlight videos. Do not leave this to chance. Know that you have some way of making these two videos. Do not depend on your high school coach. Have a sure plan in the works now. Make arrangements with your high school coach to get your hands on the full game tapes. If that isn't possible, make the tapes yourself. The point is, these highlight videos are critical to the recruiting process.

Many high school coaches do not want to take the time to do these types of extra things so offer to pay him for his trouble if you need to. Do whatever you need to do to get high quality footage of your games. High quality game tapes equal excellent quality highlight videos. For the most part, college coaches will discard poor quality videos.

If you did not take any game day visits as a junior, college football coaches usually send out three game day tickets to recruiting prospects the first two weeks in August - one ticket for you and two for your parents. These are treated as unofficial visits. Plan to make some of these unofficial visits and for sure make the ones that are nearby where you live. Be cautious of making unofficial visits clear across the country as the travel expenses really add up, and they may turn out to be unimportant to any particular recruiting process.

NOTE: It is your responsibility as a student/athlete to read the NCAA rules and recruiting guidelines to ensure that you are always in compliance. They do change frequently, so it is essential that you review them every year. Additionally, you should also read the NCAA guidelines for coaches to ensure that they too are in compliance when they make contact with you.

Chapter 30

SENIOR ~ SEPTEMBER

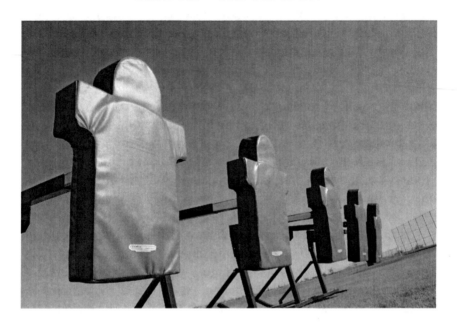

Recruiting Program

If you have waited until your senior year to start your recruiting process, as we have already said, you are at a distinct disadvantage since by now, most of your competition has already completed many of the recruiting steps we talk about in this book. But if you have talent, it may still not be too late.

The first step is to make a Recruiting Profile composed of your contact information, grades and academic information, honest athletic accomplishments and a picture. You must do this immediately; there is no time to waste. Instructions and a sample are in the Appendix of this book.

Next, you and your parents need to work together to find a list of colleges or universities that fit you athletically, socially, and academically. These will become the schools on your wish list. Make sure that all the schools on your wish list have the courses you need to complete a major in your chosen field. Many college freshmen don't know yet what they what to do as a career, so if that it is case, don't worry about it at this time.

Develop a wish list of at least twenty-five to forty schools. Make sure that schools from all division levels are on the list. Even though you may think you are destined for bowl level play, do not just focus on D-I schools.

Aggressively market yourself to the college coaches at all the schools on your wish list. Among other things, you will write them an introductory Email telling them of your interest in playing football for their school. Attach your recruiting profile and a link to your highlight video if you already have one. If you do not yet have a video, as soon as you do get one, send another Email to all the coaches with a link to your video.

Since you are racing against time, make sure that your profile is on Rivals, Scout, 247Sports, and ESPN if possible. Build or have someone make you a personal athletic website. Post your profile, videos and updates to this site. Instructions for making the personal website are in the Appendix of this book.

Then you will either make or have made high quality highlight videos. This is a very important step in the recruiting process as it shows college coaches what you can do. Most college coaches do not have the funding to travel around the country to actually see potential recruits play so they do depend on seeing good highlight videos.

As soon as you have a highlight video of your first three games, post it to YouTube and have it added to the sites above where you have your recruiting profile. You want it available online in as many places as possible in case a coach wants to look at it.

The Internet makes it very convenient for coaches to see all of your information within a few seconds. You can either Email a link or tell the coach over the phone where he can locate all your up-to-date information. Instructions for the video and personal athletic website are in the Appendix.

Year To Showcase Your Talent

This year will, no doubt, be best and most fun year of your high school career. Everyone will be looking up to you and you will be feeling pretty good about all the attention. It will be very easy to take your mind off your main goal, which is to receive a college football scholarship. Giving yourself the best opportunity to put yourself in the race for one of those sought-after scholarships means giving your very best on the football field this year.

What exactly does that mean? It means leaving nothing on the football field every single play. Since college football coaches will be requesting the first three game tapes of this year's season from some of you, you must bring it every play and that is true even if you are playing both sides of the ball and are also on a special teams unit.

The coaches will be looking for you to play off and take shortcuts. If you do this on your high school team, they will think that you will do the same thing at the college level. You must prove to them that you are a hard working athlete whether you are hitting the weights or rushing your opponents during the heat of the game.

If you are fortunate enough to get a request from a coach for full game tapes, you can assume that the coach is interested in you for his team. Because of time constraints, taking the time to watch a full game tape is a big deal to a college coach. Be prepared to send out the tapes. Either arrange to get them from your high school coach, or make them yourself. If a coach has not requested these tapes, don't bother sending it cold. It probably won't be watched.

September 1st Brings Exciting Changes In Recruiting

As of September 1, college coaches can now call you once per week. They also could have called you from April 15th – May 31, during spring evaluation, last year, but the calls were severely limited then. Each coach was allowed only one call then.

Official visits to college campuses can now begin as of September 1. While they can legally be taken as of this date, most coaches will wait until later in the fall or even the winter before they give much attention to official visits. This is because they are busy with their own seasons. There is enormous pressure on college football coaches to win games. So until after their football season is over, while recruiting is important, it is not as important as finishing out their own season on the winning side.

Make unofficial visits to some schools on your wish list. If you have let the college coaches know when you will be attending their games, by NCAA rules, they can provide you with three tickets. One for you and two for your parents or whomever else you would like to take.

During the unofficial visit, get to the campus early enough to tour the campus and have a quick chat with the coach. Remember, he has a game that day so there won't be a lot of time from him. But he will probably spend a couple of minutes with you, which gives him a perfect opportunity to look you over and do the famous 'eyeball' test if he hasn't already done one.

These unofficial visits may be even more important as far as recruiting goes than official visits because they give you the opportunity to be on campus during game days. They give you the best idea of what it would be like to actually attend the school. Official visits are tightly scheduled and they are typically in December after the football season is over.

If an unofficial visit involves a plan ticket, then the best rule of thumb is to wait to make the visit until you receive an official invite to travel that distance. A long distance trip like this could easily cost your family $1,000 or more when the cost of a motel, rental car, plane ticket and meals are added in. For that reason, most athletes should make the trips that are within no more than five hours distance from their homes. While your family pays for Unofficial visits, Official visits are paid for by the university.

Here are some questions to ask yourself after you have made one of the unofficial visits:

- Can you see yourself fitting in at the school? Was it too large or too small? If it was a D-III school, the game day atmosphere may not be as impressive as even one of your high school games.
- How did the football coaches behave toward you? While it is game day for them, you can still probably get a good feeling for your importance to them by the amount of attention they pay you. There may be time for you to ask questions of the coaches during this visit.

Remember, these unofficial visits do not mean all that much as far as your recruiting process goes. Just because the coach has given you three free tickets to a game does not mean that he is recruiting you for his team. Many coaches send these tickets out in mass.

Have You Taken Your ACT/SAT's?

If you haven't yet taken them, then do so as soon as possible. Hopefully, your GPA is good enough as you don't have a lot of time to bring it up, but if your grade point average is borderline, you may be able to bring it up enough these last two semesters of your senior year.

NCAA Eligibility Center

If you have not already done so, register with the NCAA Eligibility Center. They must certify you if you are hoping to land a college football scholarship.

Chapter 31

SENIOR ~ OCTOBER

Crunch Time For Seniors

This is not **PANIC** time, but it definitely is **CRUNCH** time. September and the early part of October are the months to seriously assess where you are in your recruiting process. It is crucial that you make a time with your parents or other adults that are helping you and really get a realistic idea about where you are in the recruiting process. There is no time to waste!

How Is Your Personal Recruiting Game Plan Going Right Now? *Check your recruiting notebook*, if you have one, or if you don't have one, try to think back and recall any coaches that may have called you in March, April or May. Have they called you back again since school started? If they called you then, but haven't called back yet, they may have moved on, which should tell you that **you need to move on** and expand your search.

As you look at your present recruiting situation, this is not the time to flatter yourself, *be brutally honest.* For example, are you optimistically counting unofficial invites to games and form letters as serious recruiting interest? They are not; they reflect only mild interest and routine mailings.

During your senior year *coaches can call you once per week* except for a few stated off periods. So if the coach is really interested in you for his program, there is no legitimate reason why he hasn't communicated his interest to you. *Do not sit around wishing and waiting* for his call. It is late, but it is not too late to help yourself. There are some important recruiting moves (discussed below) that you can make even now to get yourself back in contention for a scholarship.

A word of caution! Even if a coach is calling you, it does not mean that you have a scholarship offer locked up, but it does indicate that he is seriously interested. However, many athletes have been left empty handed by counting on verbal indications from coaches. Unfortunately, in their zeal to hold out for the best recruits they can get, some of them will tell you what you want to hear to keep you hanging on.

NOTE: The coach, more than likely, has at least four other people on his recruiting board for your position that he is also showing serious interest in. **It is a numbers game to him**, he will only offer a scholarship to one of these players, which is why you should be applying to multiple schools and recruiting multiple different level football programs.

Check your status with the **NCAA Eligibility Center**. Be sure to update with any new ACT and SAT test scores.

If you are enjoying recruiting success, continue to **keep the interested coaches updated** with information about how you and your team are doing. Email the coaches no more than one email per week, and make your emails relevant (recent wins, yds rushed, the coaches recent win) to the coach and his program. Do not send the same email out to every coach on your list.

If you do not already have a D-1 offer on the table, make absolutely sure that you have **investigated and applied to other schools at the all the Division levels** including even the D-111 schools. Remember, if programs at any level are just *telling* you that you are in contention for a scholarship, but they haven't come through with a written offer, it means zero, zip, nothing as far as the end result is concerned.

Unsatisfied With Your Recruiting Attention?

Signing day is the first Wednesday in February, only four months away, and while this is not the time to panic, it is the time to be realistic about your prospects, and it is time to get the lead out. If you are not satisfied with the amount and kind of interest that you have been shown so far, it is time to begin again. Start over in your search for schools and broaden your scope this time.

- There are over 4000 schools in the country; you will be a fit somewhere. Obviously, if you haven't received offers by now, you can assume that you need to expand your search to include **lower level programs** in and out of state. Knuckle down and do some real research on the schools where you would be a realistic fit academically and athletically.
- Stay focused on **winning your high school football games**. It is ultra important that your team make it to the playoffs in their division. Think about it, the more games your team wins, the more opportunities you have for more college coaches to see you play. Make no mistake; doors can be opened to you just from leading your team to the state title game. Coaches that may not have even considered you before may suddenly see your talents as a possibility for their upcoming roster.
- Make some **college visits** in October, but don't make one every weekend. Save time for socializing and family.
- **Don't depend solely on your busy high school coach** for **your end of the year highlight video**. It is really best to have a quick back-up plan. Schools at the BCS/Division 1-

121

A level try to get recruiting done very early, so don't delay in getting this video completed and sent.

- Make sure the video is top quality and do some test runs on your friends computers to make sure the coaches can open it, then put it **on YouTube** so you can send any interested coaches the YouTube link. In addition, get it added to your profile on online at recruiting companies like Rivals and Scouts. Also remember to add it to you own personal recruiting website and to your Facebook page.
- Have a **full game tape available** ahead of time in case some college coach would like to see one. Do not wait until the last minute to get these videos. Having them on hand could mean the difference between your getting an offer or not.

Finalize Your List of Schools

Of course, you want to obtain a college football scholarship, but remember your overall goal should be to get a college education in your field of interest. Do the schools that are recruiting you offer programs that will meet your academic requirements? Get together with your family and settle on those schools that offer a degree in your field. Focus all your recruiting focus on these schools.

Chapter 32

SENIOR ~ NOVEMBER

Time To Get The Big Picture!

You are not just competing for a football scholarship against the athletes in your city, or even your state. You are competing against football players **from high schools all across the country**, and now via the Internet all over the world.

Only the 120 NCAA D-1A schools guarantee full ride scholarships. These schools will offer yearly from **2400 to 2760 full ride scholarships**. To put this in perspective for you, there are some 127,000 athletes that want to go on to play college football every year.

These numbers should tell you that **most high school recruits** will be getting scholarships at schools that are not required to offer full ride scholarships.

With those numbers in mind, it is **crucial for senior football recruits** to focus on finishing their recruiting process in a good solid position. If you have not already done so, **this is the last season you will have to give the coaches the impressive numbers** that convince them that you are scholarship material.

Why The Playoffs Are Important To Senior Recruits!

- *They give you a chance to put up better numbers.* The number one thing you can do is to help your team make it to the state playoffs. Why? Again it is a numbers game, the more games you play, the more opportunities there will be for you to put up the numbers that could ratchet up the coaches interest enough to make them want to watch your highlight video.
- *There will be many more college recruiters, scouts and coaches attending these games.* This is particularly true of the state playoff game; they make it a priority to attend these games.
- *The college coaches know that the playoff games are the best places to see athletes play under pressure* and they realize that these games are often the first time that many high school athletes will see their best competition.
- *The playoffs give you a chance to grab some honors* (such as all-state), which look good on your profile.

How To Tell If A Football Program Is Really Serious About You!

- First, is there a **football scholarship on the table**?
- Are you **getting any legitimate interest** from the coaches? Are you getting any phone calls? If not, like we said last month, quit dreaming, get a move on, and broaden your search to more schools and include schools where you know you would be a fit academically and athletically. The

important thing is that you get a college education and you get it paid for, isn't it?

- In football, if a coach **talks about an 'official' visit** where your travel, room and meals are paid for, you can think you are among his top recruits, but if, on the other hand, he shies away from the topic, it is time to focus on other more promising programs where you would be a more realistic fit.

-

How To Narrow Down The Pool Of Potential Schools?

Think long range! If you have more than one scholarship offer on the table, pick the school that will most nearly let you get the education that will give you a real career in life. **<u>Remember that most college football players</u>** _DO NOT_ **<u>go on to play professionally.</u>** Additionally, what if you get hurt during your early college playing days, would you like to be just a student at the school you select?

You should have a **recruiting notebook** where you keep detailed notes about the different schools, the coaches' calls, the emails, and any snail mail you have received. If you are being recruited by several different schools, write down the impression each school made on you. Take the notebook with you on any unofficial or official visits so you can keep track of notes and what was said. This is a very useful way to focus in on the schools where you would really enjoy going.

This month is good for making **unofficial visits** to schools where you would really like to play. Don't waste your time and your parent's time and money if the school is not a realistic fit for you.

When No Coach Is Knocking On My Door, How Do I Create Interest At This Late Date?

Look at lower level schools, even the Division II and III schools, and look at many more schools, but don't desperately contact every college coach you can think of. Rather, take the time with your parents to do genuine research and only contact the schools that would be a good fit athletically and academically. Make your emails to the coaches personal using their name instead of "Dear Coach". Mention your desire to play there and any news about his school; give him the feeling that you really want to play for his team.

Develop a sense of urgency with this project keeping in mind that signing day is just around the corner, the first Wednesday in February, and while most slots have been filled, there will still be somewhere you might be a fit.

The key to being considered for these empty slots is to **get the coaches to watch your highlight video**. There may not be time to go through the channels and send videos, but you can email the coach with a link to your video on YouTube. If he is short a recruit in your position, he will welcome the opportunity to hear from you and see your talent.

Although you may have been rejected by your dream schools, **DO NOT GIVE UP**. Full ride scholarships may not be available but there are many, many more schools that offer other types of scholarships where you can still play and get your education paid for.

Chapter 33

SENIOR ~ DECEMBER

How To Benefit From Official Visits

Hopefully, you are receiving calls from coaches asking you to come for official visits early in December. They will want you to come during the first two weeks while their campuses are still alive with faculty and students. The college pays for these official visits so you should incur little out-of-pocket expense.

Here are some GREAT ways to get the most out of official visits:
Go into the visit knowing that *the coach and athletic program are putting their best foot forward*. Do not allow yourself to be pressured into anything that feels uncomfortable.

Take your recruiting notebook or just a spiral notebook and *jot down impressions* of the coaches, training staff, team members, housing and just anything about the school you would like to remember. If you are making numerous official visits, it is easy to get confused when trying to remember as recruiting comes to a close.

Eat at the cafeteria where you will be eating as a football player. Sometimes it is the same one where all the students eat, but some programs have specific eating facilities for the football team.

Inspect the dorms and off campus housing where you will be staying. Decide if you will need transportation between the housing the campus and the practice fields.

Visit the library and the area where you will be studying. Find out if the football program provides tutoring for its athletes. If they do, it indicates that while football is important, academics are important too.

Make time to meet the training staff. These people are essential to the overall success of the team. If they seem contented and professional, you can be sure that the program has good management.

Visit a class in what you think your major might be. While academics may be the last thing on your mind on an exciting visit like this, sitting in on a class will give you a better idea of what to expect as far as academics go.

Meet with one of the academic advisers. You should meet with an academic adviser during your campus visit to see if you will be able to complete your major and play football too. Your education should be your first priority regardless of how exciting it might be to play football there.

Hang out with the team members to see what campus life is really like. Also meet athletes from some of the other teams besides football. This will give you a better overall view of how athletes live and are treated on campus.

What To If You Have No Official Visits

f you aren't receiving calls to come for official visits this month, don't panic here are some actions for you to take:

Call the coaches where you have had some recruiting interest and *ask them if an official visit in January is being planned*. While this may not be your favorite thing to do, it will give you an opportunity to see where the coach stands. Could be he just doesn't bring athletes in until January.

Greatly expand your search for colleges where you would be a fit academically and athletically. If you've been trying to stay close to home, expand out of state and 3 to 4 states away if you have to. Realistically evaluate your talent, you may need to lower your expectations a Division or even two. Remember, the important thing is to get a college education and to get it paid for.

Think about how the recruiting process works, what happens when coaches leave a program after the season ends? New coaches are hustling to recruit the new class of players. The football program is somewhat in disarray until the dust settles and this may be a good time for you to get in contact with these new coaches. Committed recruits may change their minds and some top athletes may have lost interest in signing since there has been a coaching change.

Contact these coaches and send everything you've got including your recruiting profile and highlight video. You just may be the lucky athlete that benefits from a coaching change situation.

Don't Give Up! Due to the holidays and the dead period, there won't be much recruiting activity from Dec. 20th to early January. This means that if you didn't get calls from coaches in December, there may still be time to get calls in January.

Keep in mind that coaches may have up to 5 or 6 recruits on their recruiting boards for the same position. They are hoping to get their top choice, but this is not always possible. They will go down the list until they get someone signed and this process takes time. If you are near the bottom of the list, you may still be in the running, however, don't sit around waiting for the call, and get busy contacting other schools.

Division IA Recruits And Bowl Practices

If you are a Division I-A BCS recruit, December affords you a terrific opportunity to attend the practice of the team where you are signing or where you think you may sign, or if you are being recruited by several top level programs, try to attend practice sessions from all of them.

These bowl practices can benefit you in a couple of ways:
You can *compare your skills and talents to the all the current players*, but especially to the player at your position. This will give you a good idea of how you stack up and what is expected of you.

It will give you a great way to *assess the coaching style of your future position coach*. This actually could be the deciding factor in whether you sign with the school or not.

Chapter 34

SENIOR ~ JANUARY

Stay Alert

If you haven't been offered scholarships before now, you can consider the month of January to be a fast moving crapshoot as far as your recruiting success is concerned. January is always tricky; stay alert.

This month, you have to move quickly, early in the month to take all remaining official visits and both you and your parents have to be alert as to what is really going on in the minds of most college coaches.

Why? There are just too many different things that can possibly happen and most of them are based on the college coaches trying to hold out for the best players they can recruit for each position.

NOTE: It is not uncommon for the coaches to lead a potential recruit on as to whether they will actually get a scholarship and also for how much the scholarship is actually worth. When you hear phrases like:

"We love how you play".

"You are right on the fringe of being offered".

"We are going to try and get a scholarship for you".

"Be patient, you are on the list".

These and other phrases like them may be delaying tactics the coaches use to keep you hanging on while they wait for players higher on their recruiting boards to commit to their programs.

For the most part, college football coaches are still frantically juggling for the best talent they can get for next year's recruiting class. *They may have four or five athletes on their recruiting boards for each position they are recruiting.* For all you know, you may be at the bottom of each board.

They typically tell all the athletes the same promising thing, so each athlete has been led to believe he has a solid shot at a college football scholarship.

You have to hope that all the recruits above you commit to other programs. *Waiting like this is risky.* You could actually wait yourself out of any scholarship at all.

You and your parents have to be aware of what the true game of recruiting is for these coaches. If one or some of them have 'said' they want you to play for their programs, but you have received no official offer, then move on to other and lower level programs.

If you have been recruiting Division 1-A schools, drop to Division 1-AA and Division 2 schools. *It is now or never time.* Get all your information out to these new schools; do not wait for coaches on your wish list to offer; the offer may not be forthcoming.

Late January Means Fewer Scholarship Dollars

Naturally, *as the days tick by in January and it gets closer to signing day, the scholarship dollars available become fewer and fewer.* Suppose a coach has 'told' you that he wants you to play for his team, but he waits until late January to bring you in for the official visit where he will offer you a scholarship.

But, by that time, because he has already spent most of his scholarship budget, **he may only be able to offer a 10% scholarship instead of the 100% contrac**t you imagined you would be getting. Where will you get the other money you need to pay for your education? This could be a good time to drop a Division level in order to get a larger scholarship offer.

A good way to monitor where your competitors are committing is through websites like Scouts and Rivals.
Doing The Right Thing

When you do commit, place a call to the other schools that have been recruiting you and tell them the situation. While it may be a difficult call since you may have developed relationships with some of these coaches, it is the honorable thing to do and they will appreciate the update.

Before Committing To Any School

If you are lucky enough to have offers from more than one school, **get out your recruiting notebook** or assemble all the notes you have made throughout the recruiting process and go over everything with your parents or whoever has been helping you.

While the final decision should be yours, **take your parents and possibly your high school coach's feedback into mind too**.

Base your **decision on where you can get the best education for your future** and not on where your friends' think would be cool.

National Letter Of Intent
The National Letter Of Intent or the NLI program is administered through the NCAA Eligibility Center. Specific questions regarding its application should be directed to the NLI office at 317-223-0706. Additional information, including frequently asked

questions, can be obtained through the NLI Program website at http://www.national-letter.org.

What Is The National Letter Of Intent?

It is a legal and binding agreement between a prospective student/athlete and an institution in which the institution agrees to provide the student/athlete who is admitted to the institution and is eligible for financial aid under the NCAA rules athletic aid for a specified period of time in exchange for the prospect's agreement to attend the institution.

NOTE: You are signing the agreement with the institution and not the coach who recruited you therefore, you should ask yourself if you would still like to attend the school if the coach moved on.

While you may have established a good relationship with the coach during the recruiting process, be sure that you are choosing the school for other solid reasons like is it the best place to get your education?

While you may change your mind about committing before you sign the NLI, once you sign with an institution, you cannot change your mind without stiff penalties. If you do not attend the institution or you transfer before one year is completed, you will lose a year of playing eligibility. Think long and hard before you sign this document.

Another Legal Point

In most cases, you will likely play football at the school where you sign the NLI, but signing it does not guarantee you either a spot on the team or playing time. Again, you are signing a contract stating that you will attend the institution and not that you will play on the team at a certain position.

Things To Do This Month

Finish taking your five official visits. The coaches and staff will be buttering you up. Sniff out any negatives while on the visits.

Make your final school decision if at all possible. If you don't have offers on the table, start calling coaches and sending out all your information to new schools. Keep calling as you may luck out if coaches haven't gotten commitments from their top pick athletes.

There will be a lot of recruiting hoopla, make sure that you don't neglect your grades and GPA.

Update your athletic website regularly. If you haven't been offered a scholarship yet, this site will be a quick and easy way for your highlight video to be seen by prospective coaches.

Lastly, keep your nose clean and stay out of trouble, you've come too far to mess up now.

Chapter 35

SENIOR ~ FEBRUARY

Last Ditch Time For Football Recruits Or Pat Yourself On The Back

Hopefully, you have a college football scholarship offer on the table; if you're one of the sought-after recruits, you may even have several offers to choose from. You are definitely one of the lucky ones in the entire US. If you got the offer you wanted, all the hard work of both you and your parents has finally paid off.

The stress is over now. Congratulations to all of you, you deserve to be commended on a job well done. You'll be getting to play football the next four years at the collegiate level and you'll have your college education paid for.

What a memorable, exhilarating experience of a lifetime. It is something that you will never forget. Pat yourself on the back, you are home free, you are in the enviable position of sitting down at the signing table.

Signing Your National Letter Of Intent

The first day you can sign the National Letter Of Intent is the first Wednesday in February, which is February 1st this year, but the signing period goes through April 1, 2013. If you have several offers and you are still undecided, be absolutely sure of your choice BEFORE you sign the NLI.

You can change your mind after a verbal commitment to a coach, but football recruits suffer heavy penalties for changing their minds after signing the NLI. Discuss this binding contract carefully with your parents BEFORE you sign it.

What To Do If No Offers Are On The Table

If you didn't get an offer, it will be a scramble for you. Occasionally during this month, a hot prospect will fall through for a coach and he may want to recruit you as a last minute replacement for his first choice recruit, but don't count on this happening. It is a possibility, but it is not a reason to sit back and wait.
This is the time to get off your behind and get busy and do everything you can to get yourself recruited.

Consider walk-on spots and start calling coaches and keep calling coaches at all levels. Be proactive on a national level in looking for spots that have not been filled.

Do not rule out the Division 3 schools. Here is why. While coaches at D-III schools do not have scholarships to offer, those schools often come up with interesting and creative ways to reduce tuition expenses for players they really want in their football programs.

The D-3 schools should not be omitted as an option at this late date.

As we've just said, *coaches may have vacant spots* now because athletes they were hoping to sign for certain positions actually signed with other schools.

If you are talented and have the grades you may still have an excellent chance of signing with a D-II school. The D-II school coaches are waiting to see which athletes signed with D-I schools so they may absolutely have more slots available right now. Get your information to these schools.

You should have been recruiting schools from the various levels already; however, *if you concentrated only on the big D-I state schools, now is the time to consider some other options.* Just regroup and rinse and repeat and do everything you did for your dream schools again for the D-II, D-III, NAIA and JUCO schools.

The more coaches you call at all levels, the better your chances of finding a school where you can play football while getting your college education paid for. More than likely, there is a spot for you somewhere, don't give up.

The Advantages To No Offers
This is one of those times in your life when what you thought was a big disappointment may actually turn out to be an enormous benefit. How can that be?
Let me explain, most high school athletes dream of playing for a high profile D-I school, what they don't realize is that there is a good chance that they will be red-shirted the first year (no playing time), and *they may not play very much, if at all, the 2nd year.* This means sitting on the bench for most of two years.

On the other hand if they sign with a Division II, NAIA, or JUCO school, they will more than likely get to play all four years. So, if your passion is to play football, one of these other viable options may be a terrific situation for you. Your primary purpose should be to get a college education and get it paid for.

Division I and II Coaches Love JUCO Transfers

Junior college graduates who have played football for two years may transfer to a four-year school and begin to play football immediately with no waiting period. NOTE: Junior colleges do offer football scholarships.

D-I and other four-year school coaches love junior college transfers because they are generally bigger, stronger, faster athletes, they have proven themselves academically, they have successfully competed at the collegiate level, and they are more serious well-rounded athletes.

Junior college gives you an opportunity to mature on several levels and may just be the exceptional opportunity you need right now. Junior college graduates are a safe bet for Division I and II coaches. They are literally a goldmine for coaches.
If you haven't been recruited by any of the top schools, consider one of these very attractive other options where you may be a terrific fit, but don't delay, start immediately contacting these other types of schools.

Chapter 36

SENIOR ~ MARCH

Senior Breakout Year

As you know by now, the best scenario for any high school
football player to get recruited and land a football scholarship is to
get on the radar of the college coaches early, even as early as the
Sophomore year, but many football players, for one reason or
another, do not start to show promising ability until their senior
year.

If you are one of these senior year breakout athletes, you will have
to work like crazy to even get your highlight video watched by the
top-level programs.

If you really do have a terrific video, by all means, get it out there
to the public with the goal of garnering national attention.

Get your profile with verified measurables like your 40-yd dash,
your vertical jump, and your bench press and the link to your

highlight video posted on Rivals.com, Scouts.com, ESPN, Prep Nations, and GoBig Recruiting.

If you are really good, a Division I coach that happens to need your talent may take a look at your information.

Realistically though, you might want to consider and get your information to the Division II schools and even lower level schools. Be honest with yourself, is your dream to play football at a certain big time program more important than playing football somewhere at the collegiate level and getting your college education paid for? This is the time to answer that question in your mind.

Walking on, could be something to consider, especially if it would help you start jockeying for a scholarship next year.

You might even play for a local Junior college and then transfer to the big state school. Use your head and consider all your options. Tips To Help You Get Recruited At This Late Date

- *Develop a fantastic highlight video, use excellent quality game tape and put together a professional looking video.* At this point, the college coaches will have all but filled their rosters, if you do get few to watch your tape, make sure that it is top quality. Post your highlight tape everywhere including YouTube, Scouts, Rivals and Gobig Recruiting.
- *Create a very professional looking recruiting profile,* have it ready to send, and post it online to your personal website and to all the Internet recruiting sites like Rivals.com. Explain in the profile why you didn't get the recruiting process started earlier. For example, maybe you were injured as a junior.
- *Don't just focus on in-state schools;* broaden your list of schools to all Division levels all over the country.
- *Try to get some local media attention.* Good local publicity can work wonders.

Don't give up until you get the attention of some of the coaches. Someone, a coach at some school may be looking for an athlete just like you, but it is up to you to get your information public. They cannot sign you if they don't know about you. You must be proactive now.

Four Top Reasons Why You May Not Have A Scholarship Offer Yet

If you have done all the marketing that has been suggested in this program and you still don't have scholarship offers, one of the following reasons may explain your lack of offers.

You have estimated your playing talent to be more than it is. This, unfortunately, happens a lot of the time as parents and high school coaches are naturally biased and have placed your playing ability at a higher level than it actually is. It is a very real possibility, that you are simply not good enough for the schools where you have sent your information.

You failed to market yourself to enough schools across the country and at all levels. Quickly widen your search now.

Your highlight video is not of great quality. If your video stinks, it won't be watched. Create a top quality video from quality game tape and get it public now.

Your numbers are not good enough for the college coaches to consider you. As we said earlier, some of them look at measurables first.

Chapter 37

What Division Are You Recruiting?

By April of your senior year, if you haven't been offered a scholarship, barring a miracle, you will have to look at lower level Divisions, and at this late date, you will be lucky to obtain a scholarship anywhere. That seems brutal, but it is the plain truth.

If you have had only Division I-A eyes and have not changed your focus to Division I-AA, Division II, Division III, NAIA, and JUCO schools, you must act *NOW, NOW, NOW.*

You will have to start calling the recruiting coaches at every level to see if anyone has an open spot. This last ditch effort to get a coach interested in you will be somewhat like finding a needle in a haystack, but you could be lucky. Make sure that you have the following before you start your calling campaign:

- **Highlight Video** - This should be of excellent quality made from good quality film. See the Appendix for tips on how to make one. Post your video everywhere you can. YouTube, Scouts, Rivals, Gobig Recruiting and your own personal webpage if you have one.
- **Recruiting Profile** - Again, this should be well done with all your stats and academic information on the first page. See Appendix for an example and tips. Post your profile online at places like Rivals.com and post it on your own personal webpage.

If you find the needle, the coach that is interested in seeing your highlight video at this late date, you can give him the links to both your video and your profile.

Ask Yourself What Is Really Important

It is unfortunate, but many high school seniors do end up empty handed because they have waited and hoped for a certain big state program to recruit them. Many of you may have even waited for a walk-on position at one of these big programs, which also failed to come through.

At this point, it is good to assess why you want a college athletic scholarship. If it is to have your college education paid for, they by all means look at lower level programs.

Yes, it is true that most of the lower level programs do not have the fan base that a big state program has, but, again, examine what your long-range goals are. Is it essential for you to play in a packed out stadium, *or can you live with playing to a smaller crowd while reaching your goal of getting a college education at the same time?* With college expenses going up and up, it is worth considering.

Division III Schools

While D-III schools cannot offer athletic scholarships, they can offer you other types of grants and financial aid that in the end may end up being just as lucrative as a full ride athletic scholarship. Do not count them out. They could still be a way for you to play football and get your college education paid for.

Chapter 38

SENIOR ~ MAY

BCS Vs. FCS Schools

While there are several areas where these schools vary in the conduct of their recruiting programs, one of the main differences between these levels of NCAA football programs is the contrast in the resources.

The BCS schools have the funding and must offer every football player a full ride scholarship while the FCS schools because they have fewer recruiting dollars will offer more partial football scholarships.

The Division I-AA or FCS schools will typically not offer a scholarship before the summer of the athlete's senior year.
Why? If an FCS school makes a formal offer to an athlete early in the recruiting process, the D-IA or BCS programs will immediately be interested in checking out the prospect thinking they may have missed a potential star prospect. For this reason, the FCS schools wait as long as possible to make offers.

Since BCS schools have more money, they can typically land the cream of the crop as far as recruits go. The FCS schools are at a definite disadvantage when it comes to signing the top prospects in the country.

Backup Option Time
If you have not been recruited by now, it is definitely time to consider Div. III and JUCO schools as an alternative to the higher levels of competition.
Division III schools are not as tightly regulated by the NCAA in a number of areas. As examples, the Div. III coaches can start calling you anytime and they can call as many times as they want. If they are interested in you as a prospect, they will want to talk to you and get you into their summer football camps and on campus too.

By NCAA rules, they can offer official visits where they pick up the tab. Three free tickets to an event, transportation, meals and so forth are common. You may also participate in a workout as long as the coaches are not around.
The D-III college football coaches may not contact you or your family off campus until after your junior year.

If you do not yet have an offer, also consider playing for a JUCO school and then transferring later on. If you go this route, be sure to keep your grades up. They will count during the admittance process.

If you do not receive a full ride football scholarship, you probably should go ahead and fill out the FAFSA. All families seeking any

form of federal financial aid are required to submit this form.
There are certain restrictions for families having too much
financially or having too many assets. Here is what you will be
asked for:

Student Information:
- Marital status
- Citizenship and state residency
- Education history
- Major course of study
- Expected course workload (number of credit hours)
- Interest in student loans & work study
- Income taxes and deductions (including spouse's)
- Souse's income
- Assets
- Dependency status
- Household
- List of schools you are interested in attending

Parent Information
- Level of education
- Income taxes and deductions
- Household assets
- Number of family members
- State residency
- Age

Throughout this book, the overwhelming advice to seniors not
receiving scholarship offers from the schools they had hoped for is
to keep trying the lower level division level schools. Something
may open up for you. If that fails, you could consider JUCO and
transfer later.

APPENDIX A

Letter of Introduction or Initial Contact Email

* Sending college coaches either a letter of introduction or an initial contact email with your recruiting profile attached and a link to your highlight video makes the initial contact.

In most cases, your **Letter of Introduction**, or **Initial Contact Email** should be sent to the recruiting coordinator (go to the college websites and look him in the staff directory of the athletic site) unless you already know and have worked with a specific position coach. It should include the following:

- Be written by you with your parent's guidance and be grammatically correct using correct spelling.
- Be short and to the point, long ones will not be read.
- Tell a few things about yourself (where and what year you play) and that you have researched schools and his school is where you would like to play.
- If you already have one, attach your recruiting profile.

Briefly, these five things should be included in your Recruiting Profile:

- Contact Information including home phone, cell phone, email address (both yours and your parents), and home address. Talk to your high school coach about including his email too, **but do not include it unless you have his permission**.
- Grades and Academic Information including grade point average and any ACT or SAT scores that you have.
- Athletic accomplishments, including honest stats that you and your team have achieved.
- A smiling picture of yourself so the coaches will know you when they see you in camp or in person.

Put it in .pdf, .doc. or .xls. Most coaches can open these.

Below Is A Sample Initial Contact Letter:

November 5th, 2013
Calvin Brown, Head Football Coach
Department of Athletics
University of North America
University Town, USA 54321
Dear Coach Brown,
My name is Antonio Jones. I'm currently a junior at Little Rock
Central High School in Little Rock, AR. I am a 6'2", 206 lb.
quarterback, and will be a starter for the third year this season. I
was All-State last year and also received my school's MVP award
this past season. I have attached my recruiting profile.
I have a GPA of 3.55 in my core classes. You can contact my
current high school coach, Mr. John Smith at 501-555-5555
concerning my athletic abilities and personal characteristics.
I'm interested in attending a football camp this next summer and
would like to have more information about yours. I would like to
receive any information about your program and scholarship
opportunities. My contact information is as follows: 2222 S. Olive
St., Little Rock, AR 77777. I can be reached at 555-555-5555
usually after 3:00 p.m.
My Email is: _____.
My parents Email is: _____.
Sincerely,
Antonio Jones

APPENDIX B

Sample Recruiting Profile:

Athletes Name
Class of
Address:
Email:
Cell-Home Phone:

High School Address:

High School Head Coach:
Email   Your Picture Here
Phone:
****

Position: _____
Height: _____
Weight: _____
40 Times: _____
Bench: _____
Squat: _____
Vertical: _____
Broad Jump: _____
GPA: _____
Class Rank: _____
SAT: _____
ACT: _____
****

Statistics/Honors
Senior Year Honors:(2012)
Senior Year Stats:(2012)
Junior Year Honors:(2011)
Junior Year Stats:(2011)

APPENDIX C

Tracking Sheet:

This can just be a simple notebook with columns for the following:

A. Who have I contacted and date
B. Who is the coach
C. What did I send and when
D. Information the coach sent me

While it does not need to be complicated, it is important that you keep up with everything so that you will know who, what, and when as your college wish list increases. When you are working with only one school this isn't too difficult, but when you are working with coaches from fifteen schools, it is very hard to keep things straight.

Highlight Video Information:

One of the essential elements to a successful recruiting package is the highlight video, but typically, useful highlight video tips are hard to come by.

It doesn't matter if you are creating a football recruiting video or you are making a volleyball recruiting video, be sure to follow the tips below on how to make a highlight video that gets optimum results.

Most likely, you will not get a football scholarship without creating a quality highlight video as coaches consistently use them in recruiting college athletes. Every E-book on how to get a football scholarship, will advise a highlight video.

Additionally, football-recruiting services will either create a video for you, or require you to have one on hand. To get recruited for football, you must have a highlight video available and quite possibly you may also be required to have a full game tape.

Begin With The End Result In Mind

Before you begin, make certain you know what type of footage you want. Ask yourself, what would a college coach be looking for? What would make a good impression, what would make you as an athlete stand out?

You want to show yourself dominating and demonstrating a high level of athleticism. Choose the plays that would make a coach say, "We have to have that player." You don't need special effects or music for your college recruiting videos, you just want to make a good impression and have them like what they see enough to request a full game film.

How To Make A Quality Video:

In most cases, the coaches will trash a poor quality video. Make it easy for the coaches to watch your video and make every frame count.

On the first screen, list your name, your team's uniform color, your jersey number and your position.

Be sure to highlight where you are on the field/court - use an arrow, draw a circle or square or make a light spotlight around your jersey. The idea is to make it easy for the coaches to identify you in the video.

The video should be 4-8 minutes long.

This may be your only chance to make a good impression so put your best first three plays in the video early on right after the first frame or so with your identifying information.
- Use ONLY high quality film. No bad lighting or quality issues at all.
- Do not include different angles of the same amazing play.

Before making your highlight video, make sure that you have high quality full game highlight films to choose from.

Put the DVD in a quality package and do not write on it with an ugly black magic marker. (**NOTE**: only send via the mail sport highlight videos after they have been requested). However, you can email the coach a link to the highlight video you have posted to You Tube.

Make sure all the DVDs work prior to sending them out. Getting a bad video could easily eliminate you from the competition.

Make sure all the DVDs work prior to sending them out. Getting a bad video could easily eliminate you from the competition.

Include your recruiting profile in the package.

Include your contact information on the DVD including your home phone number, cell phone number, email address, and home address.

Also put your jersey number, height, weight, bench press, 40 time, squat, vertical jump, and anything else of major interest that might attract the coaches attention.

Using these highlight video tips will ensure that your video is the best quality and has the best possible chance of being watched by the recruiting coaches.

APPENDIX E

Letters Of Recommendation For Your College Application

Nearly all college applications require letters of recommendation. These guidelines will help you know who and how to ask for letters.

1. Ask the right people to recommend you: Many students make the mistake of getting letters from distant acquaintances who have powerful or influential positions. However, make sure the person knows you well enough to write a meaningful letter. The type of celebrity letter will backfire on you if it is seen as phony baloney. The best recommendations are those teachers, mentors and coaches you have worked with closely.

Choose someone who can speak in concrete terms about the passion and energy that you bring to your work.

2. Ask politely. Remember, you are asking for a favor. Your recommender has a right to refuse your request. Don't make the mistake of thinking it is anyone's duty to write a letter for you, and realize that these letters take a lot of time out of your recommender's already busy schedule. Most teachers of course, will write you a letter, but you should always frame your request with the appropriate "thank yous" and "gratitude".

3. Allow enough time. Don't request a letter on Thursday if it is due on Friday. Respect your recommender and give him or her a couple weeks minimum to write your letters. Your request already imposes on your recommender's time, and a last-minute request is an even greater imposition.

4. Provide Detailed Instructions. Make sure your recommenders know exactly when the letters are due and when they should be

sent. Also be sure to tell your recommenders what your goals are for college so that they can focus the letters on relevant issues.

5. Provide Stamps and Envelopes. You want to make the letter-writing process as easy as possible for your recommenders. Be sure to provide them with the appropriate pre-addressed stamped envelopes. This step also helps ensure that your letters of recommendation will get sent to the right location.

6. Don't be afraid to remind your recommenders. Some people procrastinate and others are forgetful. You don't want to nag anyone, but an occasional reminder is always a good idea if you don't think your letters have been written yet. You can accomplish this in a polite manner. Avoid a pushy statement, like, "Mrs. Jones, have you written my letter yet?" Instead, try a polite comment such as, "Mrs. Jones, I just want to thank you again for writing my letters of recommendation." If Mrs. Jones hasn't actually written the letters yet, you've now reminded her of her responsibility.
7.Send Thank You Cards. After the letters have been written and mailed, follow up with thank you notes to your recommenders. A simple card shows you value their efforts. It's a win-win situation: you end up looking mature and responsible and your recommenders feel appreciated.

APPENDIX F

General College Preparation:

Students need to be aware of both general college preparatory courses and individual school requirements as they plan their school program.

They should keep in mind, however, that these are minimum entrance standards; completion of the required high school courses does not automatically prepare students for freshman college work in every subject or in a selected major.

Students are encouraged to take high school courses that will prepare them to exceed the minimum levels of competency in reading, writing, and mathematics. It is important to keep in mind that private schools may have minimal requirements or they may be highly selective.

As a general rule of thumb, you should have: 4 years of English, 4 years of college preparatory math with one class being taken during your senior year, 4 years of a laboratory science, 4 years of history and social science and at least 2 years of a foreign language. However, make sure that you know the requirements for any school you plan to attend.

1. Become familiar with general college entrance requirements. Don't get caught with your pants down on this. It's not fun taking two math classes at the same time because you failed to notice college requirement.

2. Pursue your interests. If you have not already done so, join at least one academic, extracurricular, or social activity this month. It can be anything that you're interested in.

3. Collect college Information based on your interests. This is an excellent time to begin researching the athletic programs at the various schools where you would enjoy playing.

4. Start thinking about a career. More than likely you won't be playing your sport after college. Explore careers that interest you on the Internet.

5. Spend a day shadowing someone who works in a career that interests you.

APPENDIX G

Personal Website

Your **personal website** is primarily to give the coaches a quick way to find out about your stats, your talent and your accomplishments and it gives them easy access to your highlight videos. This website is strictly for the convenience of the coaches. Many of you will know how to put up a web page, others will need to depend on techy friends and some will have to hire it done. Whichever route you take, here some things to consider:

- The **domain name should be your own name**, for example if your name is Thomas Webster, register a domain as www.thomaswebster.com, but if that is taken register as www.thomaswebster44 (your jersey number) or websterfootball.com, or your name and your birth year.
- Remember, we said **your personal website was for the convenience of the coaches**. You can email the link to the coaches or you can tell the coaches to go to your site. Registering the domain with your name and jersey number is a great way to get him to remember you and your number.
- **Having your video online is a quick and cheap way to get your information reviewed by coaches.** Coaches can click a link and see your stats and highlight video within just seconds.
- Basically the information including your picture that you put in your profile should be posted on your website, and **you should regularly update it with new stats and accomplishments.**
-

 DO NOT PUT PERSONAL COMMENTS ON THIS WEBSITE
Post your highlight videos on your website

Thank You!

If you have gained some helpful information from this book, I would really appreciate a honest review. The information in this book has worked for countless others and it can work for you too.

Have you read our other books?

Athletic Scholarships: (Step By Step Blueprint For Playing College Sports)

How are college Athletic Scholarships offered? Contrary to what you may think, college sports recruiting is a process that you can easily implement. However, it is a system that very few high school athletes or their parents know about.

The truth is, if your dream is playing college sports, you have to be proactive in the recruiting process. Athletic Scholarships is the athlete's guide. It shows you step-by-step how to get recruited. It shows you how to get noticed by the coaches and also how to "recruit" the college coach. In short it tells you all about scholarships for athletes.

Every year, thousands of talented student athletes make the mistake of thinking the college coach will automatically come knocking on their door to recruit them. This is total myth! A college coach rarely hounds down an athlete. Not only are NCAA scholarship rules governing recruiting getting stricter, but budgets for recruiting are being severely limited by some schools.

Unfortunately, you can't sit back and wait and hope to be recruited, and you can't depend on your high school coach to take care of it for you either. Learn how to get noticed by the coaches and get on their college recruiting radar.

Find out what will help you get an offer and also what will instantly keep you from getting college sports scholarships. There are certain things you must avoid if you want to stay in the running.

One of the main keys in the process of getting recruited for these coveted athletic scholarships, is to start the process early.

Don't give up on your dreams. Start now so that you land a spot on the college team of your dreams. Do what is necessary to get recruited. Let signing day be your biggest joy, not your biggest disappointment. Whether you are interested in football recruiting and football scholarships, or any sport, this guide can take you all the way to signing day.

Becoming a college athlete with an athletic scholarship allows you to play the sport you love and get a college education at the same time.

What could be more exciting or more rewarding?

Financial Aid For College Step By Step (What To Do Month By Month & Year By Year ~ For 9th, 10th, 11th & 12th Graders)

Contrary to what you may have been told, financial aid for college expenses is available for almost anyone that really wants to get a college education. However, most high school students and their parents fall victim to the ridiculous myths that exist about how difficult it is to get the financial aid they need to pay for college tuition, books, board and other expenses.

For student/athletes that play sports, college athletic scholarships are not the only avenue for obtaining the funding you may need. Even if you do obtain one of the coveted sports scholarships, it may be only a partial.

Entering college with the money in the form of scholarships, loans, and grants is mainly a matter of starting early, investigating what's available, planning and applying for the money that is available in any given year. Above all, you cannot wait until your son or daughter is a senior in high school to start applying for the funds to meet university expenses.

"Financial Aid For College" is a financial aid book that gives you all the information you will need to ensure that your child has money for college before he enters his freshman year. This guide to scholarships lists many little known financial aid opportunities and how to apply for them. And it also explains all the many different popular financial aid sources and when and how to apply for them.

From the sophomore through the senior year in high school, you are shown on a month-by-month basis what you should be doing to make sure that the college money you need is in hand and ready when you need it. The book is written in easy-to-use language, and it leaves nothing to chance.

If you have a child who wants to go on to college after high school, and you have no idea where to start looking for the funding, this book is a must for you. It is simply the ultimate scholarship book.

Mental Toughness: (Quickly Master Your Mind & Dominate Your Opponents)

How many parents have stood helplessly by watching young athletes perform in sports only to see their own son or daughter miserably break down during the actual competition? These obvious mental lapses are due to lack of mental toughness, or what the sportscaster might announce as the inability to shake the last bad play.

Unfortunately, while most coaches' put much thought and effort into teaching playing skills and training the physical body, few put much emphasis on developing what is often described as the mental side of the game. And to make matters worse, teammates often ridicule an athlete for losing what is now termed composure under fire or what used to be called choking.

This is a strange attitude given that it is common knowledge that mental toughness is now considered more that 50% of an athletes overall performance. Why don't more coaches put more emphasis on the mental aspects of the game? Frankly, it is because they have not been taught themselves how to teach young athletes how to manage what they are thinking during the competition.

Developing mental toughness is not difficult, but it is something that takes practice just as every other aspect of your game.

Fear, is a major factor for many athletes who have difficulty staying composed throughout the competition. Others are short on confidence, and some suffer from an inability to focus and pre-game anxiety and there are also several other reasons too.

Fortunately, there are proven ways to overcome literally ever mental problem, and in "Mental Toughness – Quickly Master Your Mind & Dominate Your Opponent", you will find a check list for crushing everything from fear, to lack of confidence, to failure to focus, to losing composure under fire and everything in between. Athletes are given concrete ways to stop their minds from destroying their game before they find themselves on the slippery slope of lost composure, poor performance and losing.

With the information in this book, athletes can feel confident that they have a ready arsenal for beating any mental athletic difficulty as well as a quick reference book that can easily help them develop a mind as tough as iron.

Among all the sports mental toughness books I've seen, this short book gives you the key to mental toughness as it relates to psychology and sports. Every young athlete whether male or female should have access to this exciting mental toughness training.

Sports Camps: Guide To Kicking Butt At Sports Camp (Football, Basketball, Volleyball, Baseball & Soccer)

Are summer sports camps in the cards for your son or daughter? While most parents and student athletes know that the football summer camps, basketball camps, and volleyball summer sports camps and other sports camps do exist, not many people realize just how very important attending just one sport camp can be to the process of being offered a lucrative college athletic scholarship.

The fact is, that almost every high school athlete that gets recruited to play college sports has attended one and many have attended numerous summer sports camps during their high school playing career. The value of the university and college sport camps simply cannot be overlooked if a college career in sports is the ultimate goal.

Sports recruiting experts all agree that sports camps are a critical part of the recruiting process. While they do give the young athlete, either male or female, the opportunity to develop skills and improve performance, and they also let the athlete pit his or her skills and talents against different and sometimes more advanced athletes; the main thing they do is give the hopeful college recruit the vital college coach EXPOSURE they need to actually get recruited.

Unfortunately, many student athletes and their parents do not adequately prepare to get the most out of the athletic summer camps; they typically see them as just something to do in the summer. Such an attitude toward the sports camps is a huge mistake. Actually, attending just one sport camp and making a good impression could be the ticket to a college sports scholarship.

How To Kick Butt At Sports Camp shows you exactly how to make the most of your summer camp experience; it shows you exactly how to excel at camp and how to get the college coaches to notice you.

This little book shows you in simple easy-to-understand language how to:

Prepare for camp the correct way so you can excel easily.
Behave at camp to make a good impression on the coaching staff.
Take your friends with you to play college sports.

Take advantage of camp sponsored MVP scholarship.
Evaluate the different types of camps for maximum benefit.
Size up the sports camp coaching staff to take advantage of their particular expertise.
Pay for your summer sports camps in innovative ways.
Attend multiple summer camps so you can get a college athletic scholarship to play your sport in college.

Read this book before you make the decision to attend a sports camp this summer, you will be glad you did.

Financial Aid For College Step By Step (What To Do Month By Month & Year By Year ~ For 9th, 10th, 11th & 12th Graders)

Did you know that paying for college could be as simple as having a decent GPA? We all know the price of a college education is going up every year. With the present state of the economy, how many families can afford to pick up the price tag of from $60,000 to well over a $100,000 to send each one of their children to college? Not many, of that I can assure you.

Parents, though willing, simply cannot do it, so where will the money come from? Now, more than ever before, your child's academic performance in high school can mean the difference between getting a higher education or not.

Most high school students and their parents know that academics are important, but it is clear from the low academic scores all across the country that many do not really realize that a good GPA combined with acceptable ACT/SAT scores and well-written essays are really the admittance TICKET for college.

Good grades are a free passage to college regardless of how rich or how low on cash a family may be. If you maintain a solid GPA, score well on your SAT/ACT and have a decent essay; you will be admitted to college. It is as simple as that. There is no excuse in the U. S. for anyone not getting a higher education if they really want one.

Typically, both parents and their high school age students fail to recognize the benefits of good study habits and making good grades until it is almost too late. There may be a last ditch effort during the first semester of the senior year to start bringing the grades up, but this late effort is usually not enough.

Beginning with the ninth grade and going through the twelfth grade " Paying For College – What To Do Academically" guides your high school student through to academic success so that when the time comes to enter college, he or she will have the academic record it takes to be admitted and they will also be ready to do well in college level courses.

This book will appeal to your son or daughter's sense of pride and responsibility toward their classes. When they actually realize that their daily attention to their studies can be their free ticket to a college education, they suddenly begin to focus on their academics in a new and productive way. They are given the tools the need to develop sound study habits, to do well on ACT/SAT tests, and they are guided through the process of writing essays that will be approved by college admittance committees.

A solid high school academic record is like having a huge college savings fund. It relieves parents of the considerable financial burden of having to pay for college out-of-pocket, and it gives your child a fantastic opportunity to take responsibility for paying his or her way through college. This book empowers high school students to take charge of their high school academics so that college admittance is something to be counted upon rather than something to worry about.

Be sure to visit our blog http://college-athletic-scholarship.com for additional information on athletic scholarships and free giveaways.

Wishing you all the best,

Lynn West & Athletic Scholarship Info

CPSIA information can be obtained at www.ICGtesting.com
Printed in the USA
LVOW11s1926020414

380032LV00015B/1153/P